HURRICANE SURVIVAL

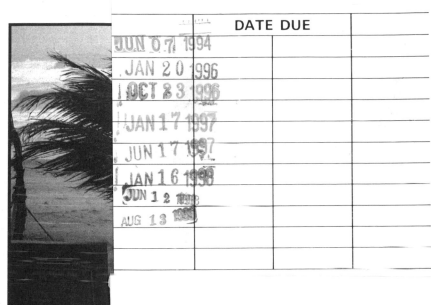

H...   ...amily
and   ...rricane

FORT LAUDERDALE, FLORIDA

TRIBUNE
PUBLISHING
ORLANDO, FLORIDA
1993

EXECUTIVE EDITOR
John Christie

EDITOR
Philip Ward

DESIGN EDITOR
Betsy Flagler Washburn

ASSOCIATE EDITORS
Roy Wenzl/text
Lynn Occhiuzzo/graphics
Jerry Lower/photographs

WRITERS
Seth Borenstein
Alan Cherry
A.D. Burch
Eric Conrad
Donna Pazdera
Robert McCabe
Doreen Christensen

GRAPHICS
Bonnie Lallky-Seibert
Theresa Albrecht

COPY EDITOR
Jim Tolpin

RESEARCH
MaryAnn McCarthy
R.J. Petrovich
Dottie Horrocks

PHOTO IMAGING
Robert Cauvel
Karin Devendorf
Glenn Kirchhoff
Michael Matute
Son Viet Pham

SPECIAL ASSISTANCE
Tony Majeri, *Chicago Tribune*
Jim Bostwick
Bill Henderson
Hayes Johnson
Lynn Ross

SUN-SENTINEL
Publisher and President:
Thomas P. O'Donnell
Editor: Gene Cryer
Managing Editor: Earl Maucker

TRIBUNE PUBLISHING
Editorial Director: George C. Biggers III
Managing Editor: Dixie Kasper
Senior Editor: Kathleen M. Kiely
Production Editor: Ken Paskman

For information:
Tribune Publishing
P.O. Box 1100
Orlando, Fla. 32802-1100
800-788-1225

Printed in the United States, 1993.

ISBN 0-941263-99-1

COVER PHOTOGRAPH: Phil Skinner
Daylight breaks on the beach in Boca Raton, Florida, after Hurricane Andrew.
BACK COVER PHOTOGRAPH: Mark Randall
Bill Layne and Bart Trank of Delray Beach, Florida, put up hurricane shutters as Andrew approaches.

At 5 a.m. August 24, 1992, Hurricane Andrew slammed ashore and the people of South Florida confronted one of the worst disasters in our history.

The Sun-Sentinel *covered the story around the clock — the preparations before, the fury of the storm, the aftermath.*

We are still covering the story and will be for years to come.

The lessons already learned, by us and by our readers, form the basis of this book.

It is your guide to preparing for — and surviving — the next hurricane.

Gene Cryer
Editor, *Sun-Sentinel*

Robert Sheets, left, director of the National Hurricane Center in Coral Gables, Florida, and hurricane specialist Hal Gerrish plot the path of Hugo in 1989.

THE ASSOCIATED PRESS

Hurricane Andrew proved you must be prepared.

All the work we do at the National Hurricane Center — tracking storms, predicting where they will go and how strong they will be, and issuing watches and warnings — means little if you don't prepare.

People who have experienced a hurricane firsthand usually take them seriously ever after, and they prepare.

Fortunately, the vast majority of the people who live along our highly developed — and highly vulnerable — coastlines have not experienced a hurricane.

However, the chances are high that someday they will experience the devastation of a major hurricane. It could happen this year.

On average, three hurricanes hit the United States every two years. History tells us that we will soon be entering a period of even more frequent, and stronger, hurricanes.

In fact, we may already be in that period: We had Gilbert in 1988, Hugo in 1989, Bob in 1991, and Andrew in 1992. All were severe, destructive storms. And there will be more.

If you are going to live in hurricane-prone areas, you must prepare to deal with hurricanes.

Books like this one produced by the *Sun-Sentinel* can help substitute education for experience, and make you better prepared in case you're ever in the path of a hurricane. ■

Robert C. Sheets

Robert C. Sheets
Director
National Hurricane Center
Coral Gables, Florida

GETTING READY

Don't wait until your neighbors start boarding their windows. Don't wait for the TV weather forecaster to interrupt your favorite program.

Don't even wait for hurricane season, which runs June 1 through November.

The chances of surviving the next hurricane – and of saving your possessions – improve significantly if you take action now.

Why bother? Consider what you're up against:

If you took the energy an intense hurricane generates in one day and converted it to electricity, you could supply the electrical needs of the entire United States for six months.

A storm with that kind of power killed half-a-million people in Bangladesh in 1970. Twenty-one years later, another powerful storm killed 150,000 more Bangladeshis.

The unnamed hurricane that struck Galveston, Texas, in 1900 killed at least 6,000 people. Since 1900, hurricanes have killed at least 13,100 people in the United States, including 3,000 in Florida.

Hurricanes are deadly, but with improved forecasting, more and earlier warnings and instantaneous communication, death tolls in the United States have

With Andrew bearing down in August 1992, Geoffrey Gebaide puts up an awning before leaving his mobile home in Davie, Florida. Because of warnings, hurricanes are the most survivable of natural disasters. But you must take precautions.

JACKIE BELL

dropped dramatically, from 8,100 between 1900 and 1910 to only 125 in the 1980s.

Property damage, though, is on the rise, in large part because there's so much more to destroy. Calculations using 1990 dollars show that in the 1920s, hurricanes caused $2 billion in damage. In the 1980s, the figure was up to $15 billion. And in the first three years of this decade, the damage toll has already hit $22 billion.

Damages will continue to rise, said Robert Sheets, director of the National Hurricane Center, as long as people insist on living and building in hurricane-prone areas.

But people don't have to die.

Hurricanes, despite their destructive power, are the most survivable of natural disasters. With an earthquake, you get virtually no warning. With a tornado, you get maybe 10 minutes. But with a hurricane, you have at least a day to prepare.

One day, of course, is not enough time. To properly prepare for a hurricane, you need to start now, long before a hurricane threatens. And coloring all your plans should be this realization: After a hurricane, help may not arrive for weeks.

Kate Hale, director of the Dade County Emergency Management Office, says that whether you survive is essentially up to you.

"People have really got to understand how really, really critical it is to be independently capable of survival," she says.

Start by protecting your home. It is your biggest investment and, assuming you don't live in an evacuation area, your likely place of refuge.

Coverings for windows and sliding glass doors are critical.

The strength of your roof can make the difference between light damage and devastation.

Now is also the time to read your homeowners policy and touch base with your insurance agent. Do you have replacement-value insurance on your property? Has your policy kept up with the improvements you've made?

Now's the time to start getting your children familiar with the idea of a hurricane.

Now's the time to make plans for any family members who are elderly or who have special needs that require special care.

What you do before a hurricane can affect the quality of life you will enjoy during and after a hurricane.

Most important, what you do now may save your life. ∎

THE ASSOCIATED PRESS

Eric Tabbert races to board up windows at a friend's house on Galveston Island, Texas, after Tropical Storm Chantal was upgraded to a hurricane in 1989.

Two south Dade County residents console each other only hours after Andrew blasted open their home. You may be able to avoid similar devastation by inspecting your house for building flaws and making appropriate repairs.

SEAN DOUGHERTY

Andrew soured thousands of South Floridians on their home sweet home.

Although Andrew's power was undeniable, experts who sifted through the wreckage in Dade County and examined homes farther north, out of the storm's path, concluded that many homes were not built as they should have been.

Roofers' nails missed support boards. Critical roof supports cracked or rotted soon after construction. Basic design had changed over the past 20 years: Homes got prettier, but flimsier.

Homeowners should regard their homes as skeptically as they regard a used car. Check your home against these construction features:

Older homes in South Florida were better designed to withstand hurricanes than newer homes. The best hurricane designs came during the 1950s and 1960s: one-story, concrete block homes with small windows, doors that open out instead of in and hipped roofs. A hipped roof slopes in every direction, with no large, flat surfaces to catch winds.

■ CHECKING YOUR HOME

Some of the worst designs came in the 1980s: two-story homes of wood-frame construction, with large windows and gable ends on roofs. A gable end — a flat wall beneath diagonal roof slopes — catches wind like a sail.

Inspections conducted by experts hired by the *Sun-Sentinel* after Andrew also showed that newer homes (those built after 1975) were more likely to have building flaws. More than 700,000 of the 1.09 million homes in Broward and Palm Beach counties were built after 1970.

Government inspectors in growth areas such as South Florida are so overworked that the consumer-protection process can break down. Some cities expect inspectors to do 30 or more inspections in an eight-hour day. That can mean only 16 minutes for each inspection, including the drive time.

Private building inspectors, and contractors and

Your "safe place"

Here's how to find the "safe place" where you can take refuge in your home:

■ The strongest part of your home is usually away from windows and exterior doors.

The strongest wall in a two-story home is often near the stairwell; a closet or cubicle nearby may be the safest spot.

In a one-story home, the strongest room is often a bathroom or walk-in closet near the center of the house.

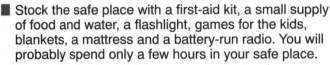

■ Stock the safe place with a first-aid kit, a small supply of food and water, a flashlight, games for the kids, blankets, a mattress and a battery-run radio. You will probably spend only a few hours in your safe place.

■ If you can afford to spend about $1,000, hire a reputable contractor who has a solid plan to reinforce your safe area, probably with wooden beams. A walk-in closet on the first floor may be the best spot. Remodeling can be done so the space serves as a safe area during hurricanes and still retains its value as a closet.

Remember:

1. A cordless phone will not work if the power has been knocked out. A cellular phone will.

2. Wear protective clothing. You may have to push through debris to leave your safe place.

3. Just in case, have some tools inside to break through debris.

4. Include a strong animal carrier to house panicking pets.

engineers who do inspections, say the already demanding workload grew 20 percent to 25 percent in South Florida after Andrew. Insurance work prompted some of the increase, of course, but most of it came from concerned homeowners who had little or no damage from Andrew; they were just getting ready for the next time.

Building codes set legal minimum standards for builders. Since Andrew, some parts of those codes criticized as lacking have been strengthened. But there are builders who sometimes don't meet the code minimums.

Although South Carolina adopted a statewide building code after Hurricane Hugo, Florida has not done so after Andrew. Builders in Broward and Dade counties operate under a different code than in the rest of Florida. Although experts are divided over which is better, most say a uniform code would make enforcement easier.

There is little recourse for homeowners who find structural problems after they move in, save for battling with the builder or warranty company, or possibly hiring a lawyer. Satisfaction is harder to attain if the builder or developer is out of business. Florida has no lemon law for homes, as it does for automobiles.

A private inspector generally charges less than $300 to examine a three-bedroom home. Two key questions to ask before hiring an inspector:

How many years have you been in the building industry? (More experience is usually better.)

Are you a member of a state or national trade group? (You want a "yes" answer.) Then, check with that trade group, the Better Business Bureau or state consumer affairs office for complaints.

Once found, many structural problems can be corrected for less than $1,000.

An example: a broken roof support, which could be a fatal flaw in a home that faces hurricane-strength winds. For a few hundred dollars, a homeowner can hire an engineer to decide what the best repair would be, and a carpenter to do the work.

Be sure to follow city and county codes when making repairs. ■

Checking your roof

Here are some tips for inspecting your roof to see if it will hold up to hurricanes:

■ When venturing into your crawl space or attic, go in the morning when it's cooler. Take a strong flashlight and step only on support beams. Nothing should be stored in your crawl space; support beams are not engineered to hold extra weight.

■ Inspect roof trusses and beams for breaks or cracks, large knots or holes and visible insect damage. Trusses or beams with those problems should be repaired or replaced. To make temporary repairs, nail 8-foot (or longer) 2-by-4s on both sides of the damaged truss or beam. Hire a builder or carpenter to make permanent repairs.

■ Check the hurricane straps, the thin, metal straps that hold the roof support system to the walls of your house. They are found on the edges of the trusses, where the trusses meet the walls of your home. Problems with loose, rusting or missing hurricane straps should be addressed by a professional builder.

■ Resin-coated nails should be used at six-inch intervals to attach plywood roofing to trusses. In some cases after Hurricane Andrew, nails in remaining parts of damaged roofs were found a foot or more apart. Such poorly attached plywood is likely to blow off under hurricane conditions, exposing the attic, entire roof and the house interior to further damage.

■ Truss

■ Support beam

■ Truss plates

■ Hurricane straps should be placed over the outer edges of trusses. The straps should be nailed to the trusses and beams with 16-penny nails and attached securely to the wood or concrete supporting walls.

Hurricane strap embedded in concrete tie beam

8-inch concrete block

■ Outside, check for cracked or missing roof tiles or loose asphalt shingles. Refasten any loose tiles with mortar or shingles with nails. On a flat gravel-and-tar roof, look for areas where the gravel surface has washed away. Scrape away any loose gravel and apply roof sealer.

■ Check boards along roof edges and gable ends for signs of decay caused by leaks. Replace any decaying boards, which typically are much darker than surrounding boards.

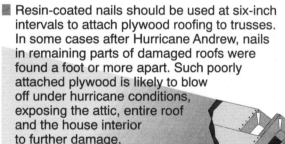

Nail
Plywood
Resin
Truss

■ Trusses and beams with knots, splits or bark still attached can indicate weak wood. Such wood does not meet building codes and should be replaced.

SOURCES: Local building inspectors, including Everett Rawlings, a certified builder and owner of Federal Building Inspections

WINDOW WISE

Protecting your windows and glass doors is a must.

Shutters offer one of the best defenses against hurricanes. Some tips:

First, find out if any special homeowners association rules regulate the types of shutters that can be put on your house, or if local building codes require a special permit to install shutters.

Later, when you're buying metal shutters, ask about the gauge of the steel or the thickness of the aluminum. Generally, the lower the gauge of the steel or the thicker the aluminum, the stronger the shutter will be.

Original installation of most shutters requires a professional; even the best-made shutters offer little protection if they are not properly installed.

It will be up to you to fasten shutters properly before a storm, so choose a type you'll be able to handle, with or without help. Make sure you can lift all the parts and attachments and install them correctly.

Remember that securing windows can take hours during a stressful time when there's much else to accomplish. It's a good idea to practice battening down shutters before hurricane season.

Here are some of the more popular kinds of shutters, all of them effective if installed properly:

Accordion shutters

Accordion shutters

Accordion shutters are mounted inside the window or door frame. The shutters, usually folded out of the way, are unfolded when a storm threatens and locked into place with a reinforcement bar. They're convenient, needing only minutes to prepare for a storm, and they require no storage.

Cost: About $350 per window, about $400 for a sliding glass door.

Aluminum awnings

Awnings are permanently attached over windows, offering year-round shade. When a storm threatens, they're lowered to cover windows and bolted to the wall at the bottom. They're convenient, requiring no storage and only minor preparations at the time of a storm.

Cost: $150 to $200 per window, $400 to $500 for a sliding glass door.

Bahama shutters

These large louvered panels can also be used year-round, though some consumers complain that Bahama shutters, even in the up position, let in very little light. They are connected by hinges at the top of the window and protrude over the bottom of the window. When a storm threatens, the protrusion rods are slipped out of place and the shutter is latched down. Some models crank down from inside the house. Bahamas

Aluminum awning

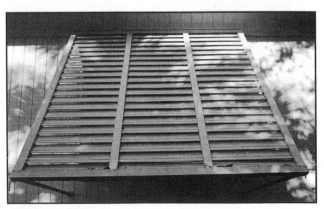

Bahama shutter

Colonial shutters

are easy to make ready for a storm but cannot be used on sliding glass, garage or entrance doors.

Cost: About $350 per window.

Colonial shutters

Colonials are permanently mounted on the sides of each window as decorations, and they fold like double doors over the windows when a storm threatens. A reinforcement bar is installed to hold the shutters in place. Easily prepared when storms threaten.

Cost: About $350 for each window, $400 for a sliding glass door.

Hurricane panels

These corrugated panels, aluminum or steel, are usually stored in a garage until needed. When a storm threatens, you take them out and slide them into a permanent track that has been mounted over each window. A bar or other reinforcing device latches the shutters down at the bottom. Highly effective, but

Hurricane panels

they take some time to put up.

Cost: About $100 per window, about $300 for a sliding glass door.

Roll-down shutters

Roll-downs, made of aluminum or tough, resilient plastic, are permanently mounted in a box or frame above each window. The shutters are lowered into place along tracks by a hand crank

Plywood shutters

Protecting windows with plywood costs about $400 for a three-bedroom house.
■ Buy plywood before the rush. Make sure it's at least a half-inch thick and rated for outdoor use.
■ Cut the plywood sheets to size for each window, allowing for an overlap. Label each panel.
■ Drill corresponding holes in the plywood and walls. Use a 1/4-inch drill bit for the wood. Use a masonry bit or carbide-tipped bit for concrete or stucco walls.
■ Hammer 1/4-inch lead sleeve anchors – not plastic – into the holes in the wall. The anchors should be at least 2 inches long.
■ When a hurricane threatens, use tapping screws at least 2 inches long to bolt the plywood in place.

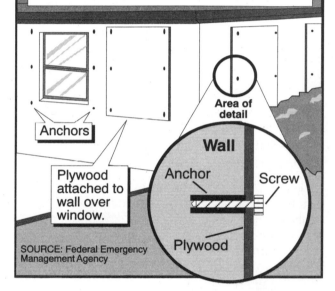

Area of detail

Anchors

Plywood attached to wall over window.

Wall

Anchor

Screw

Plywood

SOURCE: Federal Emergency Management Agency

Roll-down shutter

or electric motor. Roll-downs are perhaps the most convenient of all shutters, but they must be installed properly.

Cost: Hand-operated models run $700 to $875 for each window, about $800 to $975 for a sliding glass door. If the shutter is operated with an electric motor, add $225 per window or door. ■

SAFETY UP HIGH

Learn the essentials of protecting your condo.

❑ Remember that winds are stronger at higher elevations.

❑ Buy renters or condo insurance. The building may not be yours to lose, but you have valuables inside to protect.

❑ Choose coverings — shutters, plywood or metal panels — for your sliding glass doors and windows. If you live in a condo, does the association require a specific kind? If you rent, will your landlord provide them? Who will put them up before the storm? Get answers to those questions now.

❑ Name floor captains who have some hurricane knowledge and experience. A key duty for them is to check on residents with special needs before and after the hurricane.

Trace the route to the nearest exit stairs. That will be important if power is lost to the elevators.

❑ Designate your safest room, probably an interior bedroom, bath or hallway. Consider staying in a lower apartment or condo if you live on a higher floor.

❑ Make plans to stay farther west, at a hotel or with a friend or relative, if you live near the ocean or Intracoastal Waterway.

ELIOT J. SCHECHTER

With Andrew only a day away, workers fasten plywood to the outside of a condominium complex in Hillsboro Beach, Florida.

❑ Remove hanging plants, furniture and other loose items from your balcony or patio, and shutter, close and lock windows and doors before the hurricane hits. ■

ON THE THRESHOLD

Knowing the ins, outs of doors can improve safety.

❑ If you have doors that open out, not in, that's good. Doors that open out provide better protection against hurricanes. Unfortunately, those doors are not commonly used.

❑ All doors — wooden, metal and the large garage doors of either material — are designed to withstand high winds. But they must be properly installed and maintained.

❑ Decaying wood around doors should be replaced. Cracked jambs should be replaced or repaired. Garage doors that feel flimsy or operate poorly should be repaired or replaced by an expert. You might try replacing or making repairs to an entrance door yourself, or you can hire a carpenter for minimal cost, usually less than $100 for the labor.

❑ After your doors are in good repair, consider protecting them with shutters, as you would for windows. To get in and out, leave your strongest door unshuttered. ■

Protecting a mobile home

Never stay in a mobile home during a hurricane. Its flat sides and ends, along with its light weight, literally make it a pushover.

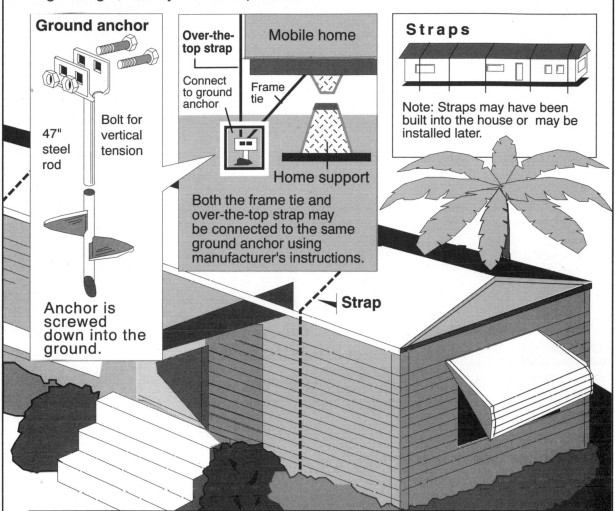

Ground anchor

47" steel rod

Bolt for vertical tension

Anchor is screwed down into the ground.

Over-the-top strap

Mobile home

Connect to ground anchor

Frame tie

Home support

Both the frame tie and over-the-top strap may be connected to the same ground anchor using manufacturer's instructions.

Straps

Note: Straps may have been built into the house or may be installed later.

Strap

To tie down a mobile home:

- Over-the-top straps keep the homes from tipping over. The straps are secured with anchors on each side.

- Frame ties made of wire rope or rust-resistant steel strapping prevent the home from tipping over. They may secure the frame, but if the home itself is not strapped down properly, the home can be blown off its tied-down frame.

- Use both over-the-top straps and frame ties to secure mobile homes 10, 12 and 14 feet wide. (Double-wides, because their width makes them more stable, usually require only frame ties.)

SOURCES: Broward County Division of Emergency Preparedness, Fleetwood Manufactured Home Installation Manual

f your eyes glaze over after a few minutes of talk about homeowners insurance, you are not alone.

But thousands of South Floridians whose homes were destroyed or damaged by Andrew would do anything to go back to the moment when they were seated next to their agent, discussing what their policy did and did not cover.

Consumers who trust their agents to cover all the bases for them when putting together a policy are asking for trouble. Get involved in the process.

Industry experts, including Florida Insurance Commissioner Tom Gallagher, insurance company officials and consumer advocates offer this advice:

■ Find a reputable agent who knows about local building codes, welcomes questions and is willing to explain things clearly and patiently. The agent should visit your home, inspect your property and present the coverages available to you.

■ Understand that all insurance policies are not created equal. Insure to the full value of your home and property. Don't make the mistake of asking your agent for the "top-of-the-line" policy, paying your premium and then considering yourself adequately protected.

Some policies offer "guaranteed replacement-cost coverage." That is the best coverage, if you can get it. Those policies promise that if your 15-year-old home is destroyed, your insurer will cover the cost of building a new one just like it.

Many people assume they have replacement-cost coverage, when in fact they have only "actual-cash-value coverage." Those policies promise that if your 15-year-old home is destroyed, you are entitled to a specified amount only.

■ Standard homeowners policies usually cover the contents of a home, up to a specified limit. Some policies protect contents on a replacement-

> *South Florida will suffer more financial damage from a large hurricane than anywhere else in the country because of the huge amount of coastal development.*

■ HOMEOWNERS INSURANCE

cost basis, entitling you to buy a new sofa if your five-year-old sofa is destroyed. An actual-cash-value policy would entitle you to only the cost of a five-year-old sofa. There are special "endorsements" or riders that could provide replacement-cost coverage for contents under the terms of an actual-cash-value homeowners policy. Other riders are available to enable you to buy more coverage for expensive items such as jewelry, furs and computer equipment.

■ There are "catches" to homeowners coverage. Blanket policies meant to provide broad coverage won't protect you. A good agent will alert you to any hazards. But don't take a chance — ask about them.

Your house, for example, may have aluminum wiring that was installed before your local government ordered that all new homes contain copper wiring. If your home is partially damaged but must be entirely rewired to meet local building codes, insurers say they are not responsible for anything more than what is provided for in the policy. You can protect yourself by buying a "code endorsement." That kind of coverage is especially important for older homes.

■ There is no such thing as "hurricane insurance." Standard homeowners policies protect you from virtually all types of damage a hurricane can inflict except one — flood, or "rising water," damage.

Flood insurance is underwritten only by the federal National Flood Insurance Program and must be purchased separately, though all licensed property and casualty agents are authorized to sell such coverage.

■ Although standard homeowners policies won't cover damage from rising water, such as from storm surge, they will cover water damage from rain driven by winds through damaged roofs or blown-out windows.

The part of a policy that offers such protection is called "windstorm coverage." After Andrew, many insurers decided to cut back on writing homeowners policies in Florida. Insurers' vulnerability to future losses because of windstorm coverage was a major factor.

To relieve the tight insurance market that resulted, particularly in South Florida, state officials did two things.

First, they created a state-sponsored insurance company to sell homeowners policies to people unable to buy a policy in the private market. The Florida Residential Property and Casualty Joint Underwriting Association, or "JUA," sells no-frills, basic homeowners policies priced about 25 percent higher than comparable policies sold by mainline insurance companies. These policies can be bought from many licensed insurance agents statewide.

Second, state officials allowed people in coastal areas of Broward and Dade counties to buy windstorm coverage from another state-sponsored insurer, the Florida Windstorm Underwriting Association. To be eligible, you have to live east of Interstate 95, or south of where I-95 ends and east of U.S. 1. Monroe County residents were already eligible for this coverage.

This coverage is about 35 percent to 40 percent more expensive than windstorm coverage sold by mainline insurance companies. It, too, can be bought from many licensed insurance agents statewide.

■ Before buying any kind of insurance, shop around. "The average consumer ... in the entire South Florida area should shop carefully for any insurance product he or she buys, because over the next couple of years, the availability and the pricing of insurance is going to vary widely from place to place and from company to company," says Ronald H. Cheshire, manager of the Florida Windstorm Underwriting Association.

■ If your home is in a flood zone as designated by the federal government, be sure to ask your agent whether you should buy additional coverage to protect you from the "50 percent rule."

The rule states that if a structure in a flood zone is 50 percent or more destroyed — by a hurricane or anything else — it must be rebuilt so that its ground floor meets minimum elevation requirements. If the front door of your home

ON THE RECORD

Making a videotape increases your security.

❑ To help speed up payment of an insurance claim, videotape or photograph all your belongings before a hurricane. Business owners should do the same with equipment in the workplace.

❑ Ideally, you should move methodically from room to room with a camcorder. As you zoom in on an object, state for the tape how much you paid for the item and where you bought it. If you're using a still camera, keep a list of item prices and where the items were bought.

❑ Keep all receipts, particularly for big-ticket items such as refrigerators, stoves, television sets, VCRs, stereos, computers, photocopiers, telephones, etc.

❑ Conduct an inventory of the contents of your closets, bureaus and storage areas. Homeowners should list everything, including shirts, socks, shoes, silverware, bath towels, bedsheets, pots, pans and gardening tools. The more documentation and detail you can provide in your claim, the faster it should be settled.

❑ Keep all lists and records in a safe place off the premises. If you make a videotape, make two copies. Update them occasionally, especially after Christmas or Hannukah. ■

stands at four feet above sea level, the government could require that your rebuilt house be twice as high or higher.

Insurers have argued that they shouldn't have to pay for raising the first floor of a structure unless specifically provided for in a policy. Ask about this. Special endorsements are available to cover elevation costs.

■ Comprehensive auto coverage should protect your car from any damage caused by a hurricane, including flood damage. Ask your agent to make sure you are adequately covered. Raising the deductible may save you money. ■

MIND YOUR BUSINESS

Get insurance coverage in order now.

The insurance needs of large companies are so complicated that firms hire experts to help them select disaster coverage. If you're one of the thousands of South Floridians who own a small business, however, you're on your own.

The best advice is culled from the Insurance Information Institute, a New York-based information clearinghouse sponsored by the insurance industry, and from other experts. They urge business owners to consider:

❑ As with any kind of insurance, choosing the right agent is probably your most critical decision. Pick someone who knows you and your business. The agent should inspect your operation and be willing to explain the coverage available to you.

❑ After choosing an agent, your main concerns should be protecting your physical plant; creating back-up systems for your financial records; and buying "business interruption" insurance to cover losses you might suffer if your business were to shut down for a while.

❑ There is no such thing as "hurricane insurance" for homeowners or businesses.

Standard business insurance policies will cover much of the structural damage inflicted by a hurricane, with the exception of flood damage.

❑ Learn the distinction between policies that offer "replacement-cost coverage" and those that insure to an "actual-cash value."

The Insurance Information Institute advises businesses to insure these types of property:

• Buildings and other structures
• Money and securities
• Records of accounts receivable
• Inventory
• Furniture, equipment and supplies
• Machinery
• Data-processing equipment and media
• Valuable papers, books and documents
• Mobile property (cars, construction equipment, etc.)
• Intangible property (trademarks, etc.)
• Boilers

❑ Business insurance policies, like homeowners insurance policies, come in many forms. Some are package deals, one-size-fits-all-type policies meant to provide the broadest possible coverage. Others have endorsements or riders to provide for a company's needs.

❑ Although your workplace may escape damage from a hurricane, you may be out of electrical power for a while. Refrigerated medicines in doctors' offices may be ruined; law firms may be unable to prepare documents; food in restaurants may spoil. Ask your agent about an "off-premises power-failure endorsement" to protect against such problems.

❑ Coordinate your policy with your partners or the officers of your corporation to avoid a coverage overlap or gap.

❑ Make sure your employees know what you expect of them. ■

ELIOT J. SCHECHTER

As son Cheyne watches, Kirk Cottrell paints message to Andrew on his Hillsboro Beach, Florida, surf shop.

MASTER PLAN

Where to go? What to do? Decide now.

You and your family should know now what you're going to do later, when the hurricane is threatening.

Your primary objective is to ensure your own and your family's survival, safety and well-being. That means making personal plans now to survive not only the storm but also the aftermath — on your own, without help, for up to a month. Here's what you should do:

❏ Decide where you want to be during a hurricane. You can stay home. You can go to a shelter, a friend's house or a hotel. You can get out of town. Each decision carries its own requirements and consequences. Study all the alternatives and decide — now — which is best for you and your family.

❏ Have backup plans for shelter. If you plan to stay home, have a place to go if there is a problem. If you are going to an emergency shelter, know which one you're supposed to go to — and know where two others are, for backup. If you're leaving town, have fall-back locations in mind.

❏ Decide now what to do if your family gets separated. Have a designated meeting place, and a backup location.

❏ Tell at least two family members who live outside your area what you're going to do in case of a hurricane. If you're leaving town, tell them where you're going. If you're staying put, let them know and try to communicate with them afterward. If you change plans, let them know.

❏ Involve all members of the family, including the children, in your preparations. Each  family member should have responsibilities so that work is shared and nothing is overlooked.

❏ Make special preparations for children. Decide now who picks them up from school during a storm threat if both parents work. Start helping them now to deal with any fears: Explain what a hurricane is, what it can do, and what preparations your family is making to contend with one.

❏ Make arrangements now for family members who are elderly or who have special needs. Remember that if someone depends on electrical life-support, there probably will be no power after a storm.

❏ If your job requires you to work during a storm, make sure now that, when the hurricane hits, at least one parent or adult relative will be at home (or in the shelter) with the children or the adults with special needs. Government agencies can require some people, such as bus drivers and police officers, to work through a storm. If you're in that category, ask your bosses now, before hurricane season, to excuse you from work to tend to children or to adults with special needs when a storm threatens. Some companies and government agencies allow emergency workers to bring their families to the job for shelter.

❏ Have some emergency cash put away. A hurricane will disrupt banking schedules. In an after-storm world with no electricity, automated teller machines and credit cards may not work. Also, prices tend to rise before and after a storm. Don't charge your credit cards to the limit: You may need them to get cash before the storm. ■

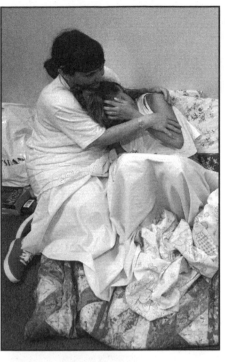

Safe at a high school shelter, Solange Orozco comforts daughter Jessica as Andrew bears down.

JACKIE BELL

PARENTS' PRIMER

Teach your children about hurricanes and their effects.

Long before hurricane season arrives, parents should begin explaining to children what hurricanes are, the dangers they pose and the safety measures to take against them. Here are some things parents can do now, before a storm threatens:

❑ Explain to your children that a hurricane is a giant, rainy windstorm, destructive and dangerous, but survivable with preparation and precaution.

❑ The more children know about the storm and safety procedures, the more confident they will be. But keep it simple; detailed information is useless if children can't digest it. Younger children, for instance, may have trouble understanding the idea of a hurricane. Talk to them instead about its effects. They need to know that a hurricane can destroy homes and leave families without food, water and electricity.

JOE RAEDLE

Lt. Col. John Hering, on duty in south Dade after Andrew, comforts Jason DeLeon, who cut his head.

❑ Using a map, help older children name the states and cities where hurricanes are likely to occur. Have them mark where you live in the hurricane zone.

❑ Ask children to make a list of what they do during a typical day. Explain to them that those activities might change if a hurricane hits: School might close; they may not get to play outside; they may have to eat different foods.

❑ It's important for children to feel they are a part of the preparations. Allow children to help pack safety kits, check hurricane shutters and plan for their pets.

❑ Children should be reminded of their hurricane lessons throughout the year; a crash course in hurricanes only hours before one arrives may cause children to panic. ∎

Latasha Walker pauses in the church next to her home in Goulds, Florida, and contemplates Andrew's destruction of her grandmother's house.

JACKIE BELL

Send away now for Sesame Street's "Big Bird Gets Ready for Hurricanes" kit. Write FEMA, P.O. Box 70274, Washington, D.C. 20024; or Children's Television Workshop, Department NH, 1 Lincoln Plaza, New York, N.Y. 10023. Or call 1-212-875-6839. The kit is free.

SPECIAL ATTENTION

Some people will need help evacuating. Plan for it.

The best way to help a person with special needs is to plan well in advance. A person with special needs is anyone who would need help evacuating in a hurricane or caring for themselves in the aftermath. That includes disabled senior citizens and anyone with a disability or serious illness.

❏ Disaster plans are required by law in nursing homes. The plans require adequate food and water, medical supplies, emergency power and staffing.

❏ Call your local Emergency Management office to register a person with special needs. Call well before a disaster because officials may need to screen you to determine the level of care needed.
• In Palm Beach County, call the Palm Beach County Emergency Management Office at 407-233-3500. Telephone service for the deaf is 407-233-3527.
• In Broward County, call the Broward County Social Services Division at 305-357-6402. The hearing-impaired should call 305-357-8545.
• Dade County residents should call the Dade County Emergency Management Office at 305-596-8735. Telephone service for the deaf is 305-595-4749.
• Monroe County residents should call Monroe County Emergency Management at 305-289-6018. Telephone service for the deaf is through the Dade number, 305-595-4749.

❏ If you require any type of life-support equipment that uses electricity, register with your local Emergency Management office, regardless of whether you live in an evacuation zone. That office can provide assistance that includes direct warning of an evacuation, help in leaving a home, transportation to a home or shelter, and transportation of equipment such as wheelchairs.

❏ Find out from your Emergency Management office whether it provides transportation to shelters or hospitals. After registering with the emergency office, keep the registration form and instructions safe.

❏ Know where your nearest shelter is, but don't report to it unless its opening has been announced by the media.

❏ Prepare a "safety" kit to take with you. It

People with these conditions or problems may need special care:
• Acute or chronic respiratory illnesses
• Heart ailments
• Unstable or juvenile diabetes
• Dependence on tube feeding
• Epilepsy
• Bed-bound
• Tracheostomies
• Urinary catheters
• Colostomies
• Dialysis-dependence

should include a blanket, pillow, folding chair, and sleeping bag or cot; food for at least two days; medication for three to seven days; personal hygiene items; identification and valuable documents (insurance, birth and marriage certificates, and special-need forms); battery operated radio; flashlight and batteries; and a change of clothes.

❏ Monitor your local radio and/or TV station when a storm threatens.

❏ If evacuation is ordered, gather your paperwork and safety kit and wait to be picked up. If the area is evacuated, your local Emergency Management office may provide transportation. Arrange for backup transportation just in case.

❏ Don't panic if you can't get a ride when a hurricane is threatening. Ask a police officer or emergency official for help. ■

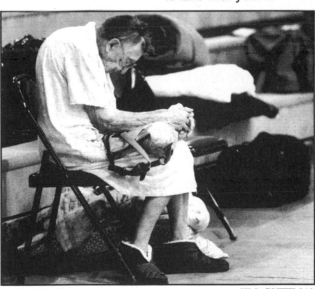

JILL GUTTMAN

As Andrew approaches, Alvena Carney of Gulf Stream, Florida, prepares to spend the night at a shelter.

PLANNING FOR PETS

Consider your options on what to do with animals.

With a hurricane bearing down, deciding what to do with your hamster or cat is an added burden.

Decide now what you will do with your pet. The choices are to keep the pet with you at home, take it with you if you evacuate, leave it with a friend or relative, or board it at a kennel. Don't plan on taking

your pet to a public emergency shelter: Because of safety and public health concerns, shelters don't allow pets, except Seeing Eye dogs. Leave pets alone at home only as a last resort.

❑ If you're going to board your pet, now's the time to call your local veterinary clinic or the Humane Society for locations of kennels. Some branches of the Humane Society board pets, but call first.

● Broward County residents can call the Humane Society of Broward County at 305-989-3977 or 305-463-4870.

● In Dade County, call the Humane Society of Greater Miami SPCA at 305-696-0800.

● In Palm Beach County, call the Peggy Adams Animal Rescue League of the Palm Beaches at 407-686-9208.

● In Monroe County, call the Monroe County Animal Shelter at 305-294-4857 or 305-292-4541.

❑ Now is also the time to call local kennels. Ask about emergency procedures and admission requirements. Many kennels require proof of vaccinations, so arrange for needed vaccinations now.

❑ Consider leaving exotic pets, such as parrots, reptiles or ferrets, with friends or relatives safely out of storm-threatened areas. Exotic pets usually require specialized care and feeding, and are more sensitive to environmental changes than dogs or cats. That can make it more difficult to improvise for them during or after a storm. For example, if a bird cage is lost or destroyed in a storm, it would be difficult to keep a parrot from

ROBERT DUYOS

Andrew left Steve Saal with only his cat, Dragon, whom shelter officials refused to let in. Make arrangements for your pets now.

escaping into the wild. Some exotics, such as boa constrictors, may not fare well on the loose, or may even pose dangers.

❑ Consider buying a portable carrier or cage to travel with household pets. The carrier should be large enough to allow the pet to stand up and turn around. If you travel with the pet, put on its collar with identification and bring a familiar towel or blanket, a supply of water and food, a leash and any medications needed.

❑ Decide now what to

do with livestock. Some animal control officials say cows and horses are better off in a pasture. Others recommend sheltering them in a stable, barn or shed. You should decide now which avenue you will take.

❑ Get identification tags now for pets and livestock. Tags increase the chances of an owner-pet reunion after a storm. Dogs and cats wear tags; snakes and lizards can be tatooed; birds wear bands. ∎

Chapter 2

THE MONTH BEFORE

It's May 1, a month before hurricane season begins.

You have 31 days for calm and careful planning. Do it now, when there is no pressure, no storm brewing.

When a storm threatens, panic will prevail. People tend to overlook things when upset or distracted, so making preparations in advance is best.

The first thing to do now? Go back to Chapter 1 and do all those things you should have already done.

Is your home as ready as you can make it? Do you have shutters or plywood for your windows yet? Have you checked your insurance coverage? How about your personal plan, and some basic hurricane instructions for the kids?

Get all that done; there's a lot more to do.

For instance, one big decision you need to make now is whether you'll stay put or make a run for it when a hurricane threatens. You also need to make plans to protect your car, boat and plane. Will you buy a generator, a chain saw, a battery-operated television? Those items can be expensive, but they could make your after-storm life easier. Decide now.

Start laying in basic food supplies.

SEAN DOUGHERTY

As Andrew approaches, Georges Nader Jr. tapes the window of his art gallery in Fort Lauderdale. Last-minute taping offers scant protection.

Trim those trees, too.

Since 1900, 13 tropical storms and four hurricanes have formed in the Atlantic Ocean, Caribbean Sea and Gulf of Mexico before hurricane season even started officially.

It's later than you think. ∎

To stay or to go.

That's the most important decision you will face when the next hurricane threatens.

It's a decision best made now, when you're calm, long before the storm.

It's a decision that may not be yours to make.

The law says that if authorities order an evacuation, you must leave if:

■ You live in an evacuation zone where there will be flooding. In general, anyone living east of the Intracoastal Waterway or anywhere in the Keys should be ready to leave for any storm. Evacuation zones are based on the size of the storm, and on expected flooding, the No. 1 cause of death in hurricanes. If you're not in an evacuation zone, you probably will not be flooded out, but that doesn't mean you will not get fierce winds.

■ You live in a mobile home. No matter how well you tie it down, it is unsafe.

You should also leave if:

■ You live in a high-rise, anywhere. Winds are much stronger at higher elevations. For example, Andrew was about 110 mph at ground level, but 175 to 180 mph just 10 stories up.

■ You know your building is unsafe and you can't repair it.

■ You use life-support equipment that requires electricity.

That's already about 1.4 million people in the four-county area who have to leave their homes during a big storm. But they will hardly be alone.

Before Andrew hit in 1992, emergency planners figured that evacuating all those who had to leave, plus those who merely wanted to leave, would take 42 hours. That is too much time, especially when you consider that the National Hurricane Center can usually give only 18 to 24 hours' warning.

Andrew made the situation even worse. Emergency planners now figure that most South Floridians, who have seen a hurricane's fury up close, will try to get out of the area altogether.

The Fort Myers area is the hardest place to evacuate, followed by southeast Louisiana, the Delmarva Peninsula making up the coastal regions of Delaware, Maryland and Virginia, and the Broward-Palm Beach-Dade County area and the Florida Keys.

■ DECIDING TO EVACUATE

Next time, some evacuees will try to leave by plane, train or bus. That's just not practical, and here's why:

■ Getting seats would require several days' notice. A hurricane evacuation order probably will come too late.

■ The high cost of making last-minute reservations for a family to board a plane or train rules out many people.

■ There are not enough seats. For example, Amtrak runs two northbound trains from Miami each day. Each has 800 seats, and many are reserved well in advance.

■ About half of the seats on commercial jetliners are reserved in advance, even during the slow months of August and September.

■ A bus is as likely as a passenger car to become stranded in a northbound traffic jam. It is unsafe to ride out a hurricane inside a bus or a car on a major highway.

Most who try to flee will resort, as usual, to their cars. But think about that. Think of 560,000 cars — more than half the number of cars registered in Broward County — on South Florida's roadways at one time.

"Evacuation would be clogged right around the Palm Beach/Martin county line," says B.T. Kennedy, director of the Division of Emergency Management in Palm Beach County. "That's where you'd have people converging from four major counties, and there are fewer north-south roads."

A post-Andrew study shows it could take up to four days to get everybody who will try to flee out of South Florida. But the exodus will not start soon enough.

"People are not going to start evacuating four days before a hurricane," says Jay Baker, a Florida State University professor who studies how humans behave in hurricanes. "Nobody's

CARL SEIBERT

As Andrew bears down, vehicles filled with people fleeing the storm back up on Florida's Turnpike. Try to decide now whether you will leave next time.

going to tell them to, so they're not going to."

On the other hand, waiting until 48 hours before the next hurricane hits will be too late. "Traffic will be backed up into their driveway," Baker says.

Kennedy sums up the problem this way: If people evacuate when they don't have to, then people who really do have to evacuate may not be able to.

Even if you do decide to flee northward, you probably will not find a hotel room. As Andrew threatened, you couldn't find a vacant hotel room from Orlando — which has more hotel rooms than anywhere in the world — to the Georgia border. People ended up without shelter, sleeping in parking lots and by the side of the road.

That, National Hurricane Center Director Bob Sheets says, is a good way to get killed. Most storms don't take the due-west path that Andrew took. In 1979, Hurricane David practically followed Interstate 95 north. You could be driving right in the path of the storm.

Think of 560,000 cars — more than half the number of cars registered in Broward County — on South Florida's roadways at one time.

Consider all this. Do not fail to prepare your home. Do not count on driving out as an option. Traffic may be so congested near home that you will realize you can't get anywhere.

If you can't ride out the storm in your home, and if you're not willing to flee three or four days in advance of any threat, then go west, away from the evacuation zones. Plan to join friends or relatives farther inland, or go to a low-rise inland hotel.

Heading inland will increase your chances of surviving the storm. But it will not guarantee your survival. Wherever you are, it will be scary, uncomfortable and dangerous.

As a last resort, go to a Red Cross hurricane shelter. The lists of shelters (see Chapter 4) often change, so call your county Emergency Management office before hurricane season and find out which three shelters are closest to you. Pick one. Choose two as backups. ■

CARL SEIBERT

Stock your car with supplies, and make sure your insurance is in order in case the car ends up a casualty.

CAR TALK

Your wheels could be your lifeline — get them ready.

Check your car insurance policy. Are you covered for wind damage? Water damage? Will the policy replace items in your car?

Keep copies of your registration papers in your car. Keep the originals in a safe place.

These are supplies you should always carry in your car:

❏ Spare tire, properly inflated.
❏ Sturdy jack, in working order.
❏ Bottled water. You can drink it or use it in an overheated radiator.

❏ Booster cables.
❏ Basic tools, including screwdrivers, wrenches and a hammer.
❏ Folding shovel, to dig you out of holes if you get stuck.
❏ Flashlight and extra batteries.
❏ Rain gear and extra clothes.
❏ Emergency flares.

If you plan to drive out of the area when a hurricane threatens, you need to plan to take:

❏ Traveler's checks. Banks and automatic tellers may be closed, out of order or out of cash.

❏ Identification. If you are going to a shelter, you will need proof of residence.
❏ Copies of important papers. Keep in a waterproof box original records of insurance, health and birth certificates; and registrations, deeds and titles.
❏ Quiet games or favorite toys for children.
❏ Medications.
❏ Blankets or sleeping bags.
❏ Canned food, can opener.
❏ Battery-powered radio.
❏ Extra batteries for flashlights and radio.
❏ First-aid kit.

It's wise to keep a first-aid kit not only in the house but in the car as well. Recommended items for a first-aid kit for the car:

❏ Waterproof container to hold first-aid supplies.
❏ First-aid manual.
❏ Sterile adhesive bandages in assorted sizes.
❏ A dozen 2-inch sterile gauze pads.
❏ A dozen 3-inch sterile gauze pads.
❏ Hypoallergenic adhesive tape.
❏ Triangular bandages.
❏ Three rolls of 2-inch sterile roller bandages.
❏ Three rolls of 3-inch sterile roller bandages.
❏ Scissors.
❏ Tweezers.
❏ Needle.
❏ Safety-razor blades.
❏ Bar of soap.
❏ Moistened towelettes, 10 packs.
❏ Antiseptic spray. ∎

CARL SEIBERT

Bruce Morton examines what's left of his Beechcraft A-36 Bonanza, flipped upside down by Andrew.

PLANE SPEAKING

Don't wing it when it comes to preparations.

Andrew flattened airplane hangars and crushed planes or scattered them about as if they were toys.

Before the next hurricane, South Florida pilots say, they'll fly their planes out of the area. That will require planning.

Two to three days' notice, at best, is all they will get.

Time may not be on your side, particularly if your family and home must also be taken care of. Some suggestions:

❑ Calculate how much time it will take to fly out of the storm's path, leave your plane and return home to board up your house and take care of your family.

❑ Deal with the house and family first, then try to fly out before it gets too windy. But that can be dangerous, particularly for less experienced pilots.

❑ Arrange ahead of time for someone else to fly your plane to safety.

❑ Store your plane in a hangar. Hangars should offer adequate protection against smaller hurricanes. Space is always limited, though, and arrangements should be made before hurricane season.

❑ Tie down the plane, though this is a last resort. There is a basic procedure, with specifics in the plane's manual.

Small aircraft usually have three built-in loops, one on each wing and at the tail. Ropes tied firmly to those loops should be anchored at the other end to the runway. But be advised: Tying down a plane probably will not hold it down in hurricane winds.

❑ Take photographs of the plane before the storm.

❑ Keep all important registration and insurance papers in a safe place. Make sure you are covered for storm damage.

❑ Know airport regulations and hurricane procedures. ∎

NAUTICAL KNOW-HOW

Get on board with safety tips for your boat.

There is no single best way to prepare your boat for a hurricane. Practical advice varies greatly, depending on the size of your vessel, availability of dock space, marina rules and local laws. Two rules, though, are universal:

Whatever preparations you are going to make, make them early. Do as much as you can now. Make a trial run.

Do not attempt, under any circumstances, to ride out a storm in your boat. No boat is worth your life. Hurricane winds, whether inland or near the beach, can lift your boat out of the water or sink it.

General tips

❑ Read your insurance policy to determine whether your boat is sufficiently protected from hurricanes.
❑ Designate someone to take care of your boat if you cannot.
❑ Make and keep a list of boat registration numbers.
❑ Obtain in advance the rope and other materials needed to secure your boat.
❑ Make sure fire extinguishers and lifesaving equipment are in good shape.
❑ Remember that when a storm threatens, you will want to remove or secure all deck gear, radio antennas, outriggers, Bimini tops, side canvas, side curtains, rafts, sails, booms, dinghies and all other objects that could blow away or cause damage.
❑ If your boat is small enough, consider keeping it in your garage.
❑ If you must tie down your boat and trailer outside, see Chapter 4.

Options to consider

Dry docking/ marinas

❑ Shop around and arrange for dry-dock space before hurricane season.
❑ If you plan to keep your boat at a marina, know the marina's rules.
❑ Many marinas have contracts that require removal of boats before a storm, though laws in some areas prohibit the enforcement of such contract provisions.

Moving inland by water

❑ Arrange now for dock space. You must have the permission of the property owner in advance.
❑ Make a trial run to ensure that your boat will fit under any fixed bridges.
❑ Take into account the higher water levels that can precede

THE ASSOCIATED PRESS

A sign in Wrightsville Beach, North Carolina, warns of possible flood damage as boaters load their vessels as Hurricane Bob nears. Don't leave preparation to the last minute.

JUDY SLOAN REICH

Even boats docked securely may get tossed about in a hurricane. So don't try to ride out a storm.

a storm.

❏ Keep in mind that cars will be top priority, so drawbridges may be locked in a down position for long periods of time.

Moving inland by trailer

❏ Make a trial run. Know how long it will take to get from the water to your destination.

❏ Consider the time required to go to the new destination and whether your route will cross the storm's path.

Flotilla plans

South Florida Water Management District officials responsible for Broward, Palm Beach and Dade counties have objected to flotilla plans, saying boats being brought inland could impede drainage, particularly if they break free and get hung up at bridges.

❏ Broward County has an organized-flotilla plan to coordinate boat traffic with the raising of bridges. Bridges are to be locked in the down

position 3½ hours after an evacuation order is issued. Flotillas will form in the area of Pier 66 to coordinate boat traffic under the 17th Street  Causeway Bridge and in the Bahia Mar area for the Las Olas Boulevard Bridge.

❏ Dade emergency management officials recommend against flotillas, in part

because the county has limited inland dock space and because a county law prohibits marinas from expelling boats before a storm. Do not use the Miami River as a refuge.

❏ Palm Beach County has few places to dock a boat inland, which could force many boaters to Broward's New River or Martin County's St. Lucie River. Get permission ahead of time to use mooring space. ∎

BACK TO BASICS

Stock up on the supplies you'll need if a storm hits.

Start now collecting the supplies that will see you through the storm. Make sure you have enough for two weeks.

Keep those goods in a place familiar to all family members. Keep them in airtight containers or plastic bags. Check the items periodically: Batteries could be dying, medical supplies could be out of date. Here are some basic items:

❑ Fire extinguisher.
❑ Gallon-size freezer bags for making ice.
❑ Clean containers for storing drinking water.
❑ Plastic gallon jugs are good. Figure you will need 4 quarts per person per day — 2 quarts for drinking and 2 quarts for sanitation.
❑ Food. Right now, you should be stocking staples, such as canned and dried goods, that will keep for a while.
❑ Tools, including

hammer and nails, axe or hatchet, crowbar, screwdrivers, pliers, duct tape and masking tape, a drill with screwdriver bits and adapters to install bolts, extra fasteners and bolts for shutters, knife, handsaw.
❑ Household bleach. Can be used for cleaning, or to purify water by adding 8 drops per gallon of water.
❑ Soap. And a plastic, covered container.
❑ Needle and thread.
❑ Whistle or air horn.
❑ Disinfectant.
❑ Hand-operated can opener.
❑ Flashlight, maybe two, with extra batteries.
❑ Radio, or battery-powered television, with extra batteries.
❑ A charcoal or gas grill, with a supply of fuel, so that you can cook if you are left without electricity or gas.
❑ First-aid supplies, including sterile adhe-

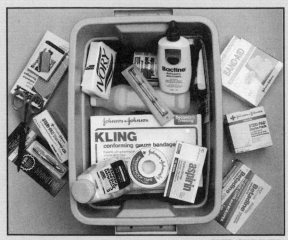

PHIL SKINNER

Items included in a basic first-aid kit.

FIRST-AID KIT
Be prepared to cope with minor medical emergencies.

Here are some things to have in your first-aid kit. Keep all these items in a waterproof container.

❑ First-aid manual.
❑ Sterile adhesive bandages in assorted sizes.
❑ A dozen 2-inch sterile gauze pads.
❑ A dozen 3-inch sterile gauze pads.
❑ Hypoallergenic adhesive tape.
❑ Three triangular bandages.
❑ Three rolls of 2-inch sterile roller bandages.
❑ Three rolls of 3-inch sterile roller bandages.
❑ Scissors.
❑ Tweezers.
❑ Needle, for sewing and removing splinters.
❑ Safety razor blades, for stripping wire, cutting boxes, etc.
❑ Bar of soap. Keep it in its own plastic bag or waterproof container.
❑ 10 packets of moistened towelettes. Or, you can keep a few wet cloths in separate plastic bags.
❑ Antiseptic spray.
❑ Hydrogen peroxide, for cleaning wounds.
❑ Rubbing alcohol.
❑ Iodine, for purifying water and disinfecting wounds.
❑ Thermometer.
❑ Petroleum jelly, to relieve burns and itching.
❑ Ointments for burns and cuts.
❑ Various sizes of safety pins.
❑ Latex gloves.
❑ Aspirin.
❑ Antacid tablets. ■

sive bandages in assorted sizes. sterile gauze pads,

❏ Disposable diapers and wipes.

❏ Extra prescription medications, enough for a month.

❏ Fuel for your generator or chain saw.

❏ Matches. Wooden kitchen matches are best. Keep them dry, in a plastic bag or a plastic film container.

❏ Eating utensils. Save water you would use for washing by using disposable plastic knives, forks and spoons. Have a two-week supply of paper plates and paper towels.

❏ Toiletries.

❏ Toilet paper. Keep it in plastic bags to keep it dry.

❏ Lantern, with extra fuel.

❏ Sterno stove, with extra fuel.

❏ Oven mitts, for handling hot cookware.

❏ Mosquito repellent.

❏ Snake-bite kit. Available at camping goods stores, some pharmacies.

❏ Water purification tablets, from camping goods stores or pharmacies.

You can also use household bleach, without the lemon scent, or 2 percent iodine to purify water.

❏ Garbage bags, several boxes, with ties, to collect refuse and store goods to keep them dry.

❏ Cat litter. For your cat or for soaking up spills.

❏ Rope or heavy cord. Get 100 feet. It can be useful in many ways, as a clothesline, for example.

❏ Tarpaulin, canvas or 6-mil plastic sheeting. Good for making temporary roof repairs or tents.

❏ A month's supply of food for your pets.

❏ Large plastic trash cans with sealable lids work well for the storage of

most items. As alternatives, try duffel bags, camping backpacks or cardboard boxes. ■

SEAN DOUGHERTY

A stocked tool box could prove useful.

TOOL BOX
Be ready for basic repairs.

What should be in your tool box:

❏ Hammer and nails.
❏ Axe or hatchet.
❏ Crowbar.
❏ Screwdrivers, both regular and Phillips head, and screws.
❏ Pliers.

❏ Duct tape and masking tape.
❏ Drill, with screwdriver bits and adapters to install bolts.
❏ Extra fasteners and bolts for shutters.
❏ Knife.
❏ Handsaw. ■

PROVISIONS
Stock your pantry for a storm.

Here are some foods you can collect now. Replace the food every six months.

❏ Canned meats and fish, such as tuna, chunk chicken or ham.
❏ Canned fruits and vegetables. You can use the liquids for cooking.
❏ Canned soups.
❏ Powdered and/or evaporated milk.

❏ Instant coffee, tea and cocoa.

❏ Pet food.
❏ Jelly and/or honey.
❏ Peanut butter.
❏ Canned pet food.
❏ Powdered drink mixes, to make bottled water more palatable.
❏ Sodas, fruit juices, vegetable juices.
❏ Bouillon cubes. ■

BIG HELP ON HAND

Major purchases could ease post-storm rigors.

If you open your wallet wide enough, you can buy some big-ticket items that could come in handy after a hurricane. Some would be useful anytime:

Generators

Prices vary from $200 for a 750-watt model that will run a few light bulbs, to $2,000 for an 8,000-watt model that will run your entire house and all your appliances. About 4,000 watts are needed to run a small air conditioner, a refrigerator and a couple of lights. Be sure you have plenty of heavy-duty extension cords to connect the generator to appliances. A generator with a fuel tank larger than 5 gallons is preferable. You'll need about 5 gallons of gas to run a generator all night.

Gas grills

Single-burner models start at $99. Consider spending an additional $50 for a model that has more than one burner. It allows you to cook more things at once. You'll need propane gas to run a gas grill, so an extra tank (about $25) could be handy. Refilling the tank with propane costs $10 to $20. One tank cooks a dozen or more meals. Mini-grills, commonly used at the beach, cost about $10, with single-meal gas tanks costing $2 each.

Camping stoves

The stoves, which cost about $60, run on small propane tanks and are sufficient for short-term use. Figure it will take about one tank of fuel to cook one meal. The stoves are small and fit easily on a shelf.

Chain saws

Small ones start at $100. Get one with a 12-to-14-inch chain. It will give two to three days of steady cutting before the chain has to be replaced. If you anticipate more cutting, buy an extra chain for about $8.

Tents

One-person models start at $30; 10-person tents start at $300. Tents can provide basic housing in a jam. The more people in a tent, the less comfortable it becomes. Consider buying more than one large tent so you can use one for

SEAN DOUGHERTY

A portable generator could run your appliances and help you minimize discomfort after a hurricane.

simple storage and the other for sleeping.

Portable toilets

Regular camping toilets are available for $60 to $150. The $60 models have a seat and a tank that holds waste. More expensive models run on batteries and flush, and they have a warning light that indicates when the tank needs to be emptied.

Tarpaulins

Tarps or plastic sheeting such as Visqueen can be handy for covering a hole in the roof or draping over valuables exposed by a storm. A 30-by-60-foot tarp costs about $80. Heavy-gauge Visqueen, 6 mils thick, costs $10 for a 250-square-foot roll.

Roofing paper

A roll of tar paper with a self-adhesive strip can be used for temporary roof repairs. The covering, which costs about $50 for 100 square feet, can last for months if properly installed. The product gets mixed reviews because it can be difficult for novices to use.

Television sets

A small battery-powered television can keep you informed after the power goes out. Black-and-white models with 4-inch screens can be found for as little as $60. ■

Trimming trees

Trees and shrubs should be trimmed before hurricane season. Don't trim once a hurricane watch or warning has been issued; trash pickup will be suspended, and the storm could turn your trimmings into dangerous missiles.

■ The canopy of a dense or vine-covered tree is too solid to allow air to pass through. Such a tree will catch and hold the wind like an umbrella. Winds will topple or uproot the tree.

■ When trimming trees, create channels through the foliage, working outward from the center of the tree, to allow for air flow. Working from the center of the tree will also help avoid the tendency to cut too much.

■ Remove limbs that are dead, weak or rubbing together. A good trim job leaves the tree looking lighter — not as if it has been pruned.

■ If you hire tree trimmers, make sure they're licensed, bonded and insured.

Hatracking

A "hatracked" tree is one that has been so heavily pruned that only stubs of branches remain.

A hatracked tree's new growth will form a dense canopy, making the tree more vulnerable to winds.

To thin dense new growth, cut off all but the strongest new shoots to encourage a new, natural branching shape. Also, remove any shoots pointing downward; new growth should point upward, against the pull of gravity.

Cutting limbs

Cut limbs at a point just before the branch collar, which is the raised and thickened area where the limb attaches to the trunk. The branch collar's wound-healing bark will help to cover over and heal the cut.

Large limbs may require three cuts to remove them safely and cleanly.

Do not stand under branch when making cut #2

GRAVITY

2

1

3
Final cut

Long branch stubs invite rot. So does thick wound "paint," which does not work well in Florida's high humidity.

Wound-healing bark "branch collar"

SOURCES: Bob Haehle, consulting horticulturalist, Florida Power and Light

David Luke, a construction manager, surveys damage after high winds spawned during the Great Storm of '93 toppled temporary bleachers at the Delray Beach Tennis Center in Delray Beach, Florida. Though not a hurricane, the storm was just as vicious, killing at least 238 people, including 44 in Florida. In South Florida, still recovering from Andrew, three people died.

MARK RANDALL

You could be inundated by storm surge, whipped by wind or stranded without power before hurricane season even starts. Those things happened to millions of people on March 13, 1993 — 80 days before the official start of hurricane season.

It wasn't a hurricane, but rather a powerful blizzard that hit the entire East Coast with the fury of a hurricane. Its nearly 20-foot storm surge and 100 mph winds were deadlier than any U.S. hurricane since Camille killed 256 in 1969. At least 238 people died in the Great Storm of '93.

People drowned in boats and in swollen tides. Mobile homes were pitched, and at least one occupant was crushed to death. Just as in a hurricane.

The storm was technically different from a hurricane. To its victims, however, the only difference was that it was cold afterward.

The deaths did not occur only up North. The Great Storm of '93 killed 44 people in Florida.

If you prepare for late-winter storms as you would for hurricanes, you can survive. If you have supplies, a properly built roof and an evacuation plan, you can survive a killer storm — no matter what kind of storm it is, no matter what season it is. ■

CARL SEIBERT

The Great Storm of '93 pounded a tent city in Naranja, Florida, nearly seven months after its residents were left homeless by Hurricane Andrew.

Hurricane tracking

To track a hurricane on the map on the back of this page, place a dot at the point where each advisory's latitude and longitude intersect. As you plot subsequent advisories, connect the dots to see the storm's travel path.

To record a hurricane's progress on the chart below, you need a storm's advisory number, date, time, latitude, longitude, distance from a certain location, forward speed, storm direction and maximum sustained winds. During hurricane season, this information will be available from the media or from the National Hurricane Center's recordings at 305-662-5702. The first line of the chart has been filled in as an example.

Advisory #	Date	Time	Latitude (N°)	Longitude (W°)	Miles away	from Location	Speed mph	Storm direction	Max winds
1	7/10	6 p.m.	25.0 N	75.5 W	98	Nassau	30	NW	120

Latitude scale (left margin): 42° 41° 40° 39° 38° 37° 36° 35° 34° 33° 32° 31° 30° 29° 28° 27° 26° 25° 24° 23° 22° 21° 20° 19° 18° 17° 16° 15° 14° 13° 12°

Storm terms

TROPICAL WAVE: A large low-pressure system in the tropics and subtropics.

TROPICAL DISTURBANCE: A group of thunderstorms that moves together through the tropics for at least 24 hours, but with no noticeable circular motion.

TROPICAL DEPRESSION: A weak storm system with winds of 38 mph or less and rotary movement only on the water's surface.

TROPICAL STORM: A storm with distinct rotary movement and winds 39 to 74 mph.

HURRICANE: A circular windstorm in tropical or subtropical climates with a defined eye and winds of at least 74 mph. Tropical cyclones, the general term for all large-scale circular windstorms in the tropics and subtropics, are called hurricanes in the Atlantic Ocean, the Caribbean, Gulf of Mexico, eastern Pacific Ocean, and near Hawaii. Tropical cyclones in the north Pacific Ocean are called typhoons.

Storm warnings

TROPICAL STORM WATCH: An advisory issued by the National Hurricane Center when tropical storm conditions, with winds of 39 to 73 mph, could threaten a coastal area within 24 to 36 hours.

TROPICAL STORM WARNING: An advisory issued when winds of 39 to 73 mph are expected. If a hurricane is expected, tropical storm warnings probably will not be issued before hurricane warnings.

HURRICANE WATCH: An advisory issued when hurricane conditions are a threat within 24 to 36 hours. Chances are 1-in-3 the center part of the watch area will be hit. There's a 1-in-4 chance any location in the watch area will be hit, a 1-in-5 chance for the edges of the watch area.

HURRICANE WARNING: An advisory that says hurricane conditions are expected in a specific area within 24 hours. That means a 1-in-2 chance the central part of the warning area will be hit, a 1-in-3 chance for the edges of the warning zone. All areas in the warning zone are likely to be affected, even if the hurricane grazes by.

Hurricane categories

Hurricanes are rated on a 1-5 scale, with 1 being the weakest. The scale was designed by two South Floridians, Herbert Saffir, a Coral Gables engineer, and Robert Simpson, former director of the National Hurricane Center. Category 3, 4 and 5 storms are considered major hurricanes.

CATEGORY 1 HURRICANE: Wind speeds of 74 to 95 mph. Storm surge is 4 to 5 feet. Barometric pressure is 28.94 inches or higher. Minimal damage, primarily to foliage, unanchored mobile homes and poorly constructed signs.

CATEGORY 2 HURRICANE: Winds of 96 to 110 mph. Storm surge is 6 to 8 feet. Barometric pressure is 28.50 to 28.93 inches. Damage moderate, mobile homes heavily damaged, some damage to roofs and windows of homes.

CATEGORY 3 HURRICANE: Winds of 111 to 130 mph. Storm surge is 9 to 12 feet. Barometric pressure is 27.91 to 28.49 inches. Damage extensive, some structural damage to buildings, foliage torn from trees and mobile homes destroyed.

CATEGORY 4 HURRICANE: Winds of 131 to 155 mph. Storm surge is 13 to 18 feet. Barometric pressure is 27.17 to 27.90 inches. Damage extreme, homes heavily damaged, complete destruction to mobile homes and large trees uprooted.

CATEGORY 5 HURRICANE: Winds greater than 155 mph. Storm surge more than 18 feet. Barometric pressure less than 27.17 inches. Damage catastrophic, small buildings blown away or overturned. Few trees left at all.

Chapter 3

HURRICANE SEASON

Any day now.

It's June 1, the official beginning of hurricane season. You should be ready for a hurricane anytime during the next six months.

By now you should have made all the preparations outlined in Chapters 1 and 2.

Don't panic; most hurricanes don't hit until August, September and October.

Then again, hurricanes have popped up as early as June. And about every 10 years, a June hurricane strikes the United States.

Be prepared for that once-in-a-decade June storm — and for the rest of the hurricane season.

Your home should be as safe as you can make it. Your basic foods and supplies should be gathered. You should have personal plans firmly in place.

You should pay more attention to what is happening in the tropics; listen more closely to the forecasts.

At this stage, you cannot afford to be unprepared. ∎

CARL SEIBERT

Andrew, which slammed South Florida in August 1992, roiled the waters of Biscayne Bay, sweeping this boat onto a street in Miami's Coconut Grove. Remember: You should be prepared for a hurricane before the season begins.

When hurricanes hit

Although hurricane season runs from June 1 to November 30, the peak of the season comes in the hottest months, from mid-August to mid-October.

SEPTEMBER
SEPTEMBER
20

Cruel September

Of all the major hurricanes that have directly hit the United States since 1900, 57 percent arrived in September.

Here's how many major hurricanes have hit, and when, since 1900:

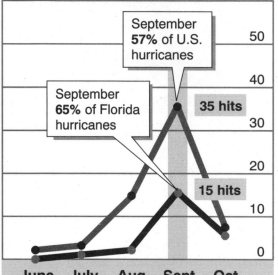

September **57%** of U.S. hurricanes

September **65%** of Florida hurricanes

35 hits

15 hits

50
40
30
20
10
0

June   July   Aug.   Sept.   Oct.

U.S. total
direct hits:
61 hurricanes

Florida total
direct hits:
23 hurricanes

Out-of-season hurricanes

Earliest hurricane:
March 7, 1908

Latest hurricane:
Dec. 31, 1954

Earliest landfall   **June 9, 1966**

Latest landfall   **Nov. 30, 1925**

SOURCE: National Hurricane Center

■ HURRICANE NAMES

People didn't always know hurricanes on a first-name basis.

In the Caribbean, storms used to be named for the saints' days on which they hit. But that fostered confusion; sometimes two storms would end up with the same name.

The idea for giving storms women's first names was conceived in the 1941 novel, *Storm*, by George Stewart, and was adopted by military meteorologists.

In 1950, the National Weather Service started using the phonetic alphabet (Able, Baker, Charlie, etc.) to name hurricanes, but in 1953 returned to women's names in alphabetical order.

To avoid sexism, the weather service started alternating men's and women's names in 1979. Names starting with Q, U, X, Y or Z are not used, because there are not enough names starting with those letters and not that many Atlantic hurricanes each year.

The names, reflecting various nationalities and ethnicities, are selected by the World Meteorological Organization and are used in six-year shifts. The 1993 names, for instance, will be reused in 1999.

A storm, once it reaches tropical storm status, gets a name that lasts the rest of its life. The names of storms that killed people or caused great damage are retired from the rotation.

Andrew was retired in 1992, the thirty-fourth name deleted from the list. ■

Here are the names to be used through the 1996 hurricane season:

1993
Arlene, Bret, Cindy, Dennis, Emily, Floyd, Gert, Harvey, Irene, Jose, Katrina, Lenny, Maria, Nate, Ophelia, Philippe, Rita, Stan, Tammy, Vince, Wilma.

1994
Alberto, Beryl, Chris, Debby, Ernesto, Florence, Gordon, Helene, Isaac, Joyce, Keith, Leslie, Michael, Nadine, Oscar, Patty, Rafael, Sandy, Tony, Valerie, William.

1995
Allison, Barry, Chantal, Dean, Erin, Felix, Gabrielle, Humberto, Iris, Jerry, Karen, Luis, Marilyn, Noel, Opal, Pablo, Roxanne, Sebastien, Tanya, Van, Wendy.

1996
Arthur, Bertha, Cesar, Diana, Edouard, Fran, Gustav, Hortense, Isidore, Josephine, Klaus, Lili, Marco, Nana, Omar, Paloma, Rene, Sally, Teddy, Vicky, Wilfred.

How hurricanes form

Florida's hurricanes are born in Africa's weather, starting as wisps of wind that can't even be noticed on the ground. The winds move from the east over warm water in the Atlantic, which strengthens them into storms. Scientists have found that a rainier season in Africa means more frequent, and stronger, storms for the eastern United States. Here's how a hurricane forms:

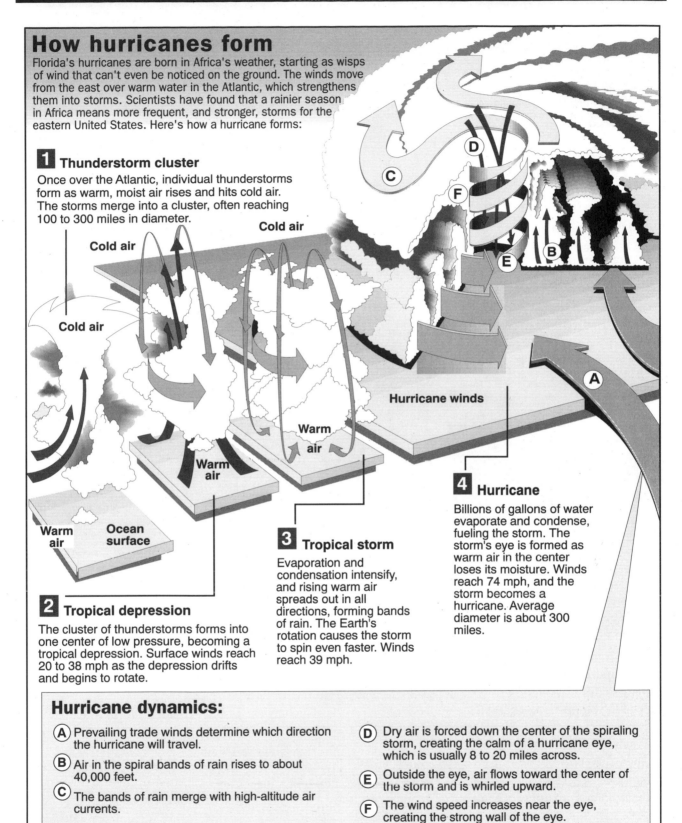

1 Thunderstorm cluster

Once over the Atlantic, individual thunderstorms form as warm, moist air rises and hits cold air. The storms merge into a cluster, often reaching 100 to 300 miles in diameter.

2 Tropical depression

The cluster of thunderstorms forms into one center of low pressure, becoming a tropical depression. Surface winds reach 20 to 38 mph as the depression drifts and begins to rotate.

3 Tropical storm

Evaporation and condensation intensify, and rising warm air spreads out in all directions, forming bands of rain. The Earth's rotation causes the storm to spin even faster. Winds reach 39 mph.

4 Hurricane

Billions of gallons of water evaporate and condense, fueling the storm. The storm's eye is formed as warm air in the center loses its moisture. Winds reach 74 mph, and the storm becomes a hurricane. Average diameter is about 300 miles.

Hurricane dynamics:

(A) Prevailing trade winds determine which direction the hurricane will travel.

(B) Air in the spiral bands of rain rises to about 40,000 feet.

(C) The bands of rain merge with high-altitude air currents.

(D) Dry air is forced down the center of the spiraling storm, creating the calm of a hurricane eye, which is usually 8 to 20 miles across.

(E) Outside the eye, air flows toward the center of the storm and is whirled upward.

(F) The wind speed increases near the eye, creating the strong wall of the eye.

SOURCES: *National Geographic* Vol. 158, No. 3; *Predicting U.S. Hurricane Spawned Destruction From West African Rainfall,* a 1991 report by William Gray and Christopher Landsea; KRT.

Hurricane storm surge

Storm surge is an abnormally rapid and high rising of the sea into a wall or dome of water that is pushed shoreward by high winds.

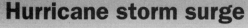

The surge, often 50 miles wide, strikes coastlines near the place where the hurricane's eye makes landfall.

Waves: Up to 30 ft.

Storm surge: Up to 17 ft.

High tide: 6 ft.

Low tide

10 ft. above sea level **Dunes**

A 17-foot surge added to the normal 6-foot tide creates a 23-foot storm tide. Battering waves and winds up to 130 mph mix with the surge to worsen the storm's effect.

■ Hurricanes often arrive with high tides and whip up large waves on top of the storm surge. During Hurricane Camille in 1969, a 25-foot storm surge — nearly as high as a three-story building — inundated the town of Pass Christian in Mississippi.

■ Storm surge can be deadly. Since 1900, about 90 percent of hurricane fatalities have been attributed to drowning in flood waters brought by the high winds. In recent years, emergency officials have been fairly successful in evacuating flood-prone areas, and drowning deaths have declined.

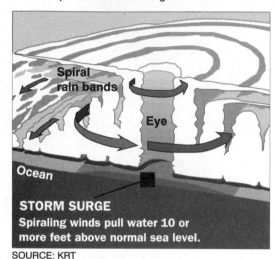

Spiral rain bands

Eye

Ocean

STORM SURGE
Spiraling winds pull water 10 or more feet above normal sea level.

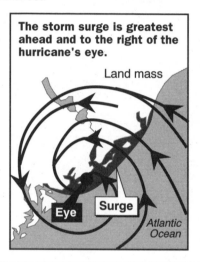

The storm surge is greatest ahead and to the right of the hurricane's eye.

Land mass

Eye **Surge**

Atlantic Ocean

SOURCE: KRT

The job of the National Hurricane Center in Coral Gables is to watch and warn.

To watch, Air Force Reserve planes and two hurricane hunter planes owned by the National Oceanic and Atmospheric Administration fly into storms to take wind, pressure, temperature and other readings from the eye and edges of hurricanes. Those readings are relayed to the hurricane center.

The hurricane center also relies on photographs from satellites, but the satellites are dying.

One of the two satellites used by the center failed in January 1989. The other, launched in February 1987, still sends pictures but ran out of fuel in 1992 and can't be adjusted in orbit.

To help out, NOAA, the center's parent agency, borrowed a satellite, which is also dying, from the European Space Agency. A new, $1.7 billion satel-

■ THE NATIONAL HURRICANE CENTER

lite won't be launched until spring 1994, at the earliest.

Doppler radar, installed in a radar tower in south Dade County in February 1993, can provide detailed pictures, but only when a hurricane is no more than 18 hours away.

The hurricane center predicts storm movements 72 hours in advance using nine computer programs.

The center can usually give 24 to 36 hours' notice for a hurricane watch, 18 to 24 hours' notice for a warning.

Even with today's technology, says Rainer Bleck, a University of Miami meteorology professor, a hurricane remains a mystery.

"It's like a spinning top," Bleck says. "You can never tell which way this thing will spin." ■

Chapter 4

UNDER THREAT

A hurricane watch has been issued for your area. The situation could quickly get worse: A hurricane warning could be issued within a few hours.

When a watch is issued, it's time to finish all preparations, and quickly.

All the plans you made in the calm of May and June — especially those for people with disabilities or serious illness — should be activated.

A hurricane watch does not guarantee you will get hit by a hurricane, but the probability is getting uncomfortably high.

Your chances of getting walloped are 1 in 4 if you live on the edges of the watch area, 1 in 3 if you're in the center of the watch area. You probably have 24 to 36 hours before the storm hits.

Monitor the storm by television, radio or weather radio. In Dade, Broward and the Upper Keys, the National Oceanic and Atmospheric Administration weather radio broadcasts at 162.550 MHz. In Palm Beach County, at 162.475 MHz. In the Lower Keys, at 162.400 MHz.

If the advisory is upgraded to a hurricane warning, you are most likely going to feel a storm, either a direct hit or a glancing blow, within 18 hours.

SUSAN G. STOCKER

A man carries water into a public shelter in Plantation, Florida, before Andrew hits. If you're going to a shelter, wait for the media to announce that it's open.

If you are in an evacuation area, you must leave. That order is usually issued by government officials soon after a hurricane warning.

If you are going to a shelter, wait until radio or television says the shelters are open. If you are staying home, finish all your indoor and outdoor preparations right away and hunker down.

Make sure you don't get caught outside when the storm hits. ∎

INSIDE INFORMATION

Get your house in order.
You could be stuck there awhile.

Here are some things to do inside your house as the storm approaches:

❏ Check medical supplies. If you don't have enough, go to the pharmacy now.

❏ Top off your food supplies. You should need only perishable goods at this point to complement your staples and canned goods.

❏ Check the first-aid kit. Replenish missing items.

❏ Check your tools. Put them all in one place.

❏ Scrub your plastic water containers with household soap, swab with bleach, rinse thoroughly, let dry. Then fill the containers with water.

❏ Turn refrigerator and freezer to the coldest settings. Start freezing plastic gallon-size freezer bags and 2-liter soda bottles almost filled with water. Do not open the refrigerator unless you absolutely have to. A portable ice chest can be used as a substitute to keep food and beverages cool.

❏ Identify where you shut off gas, water and electricity.

❏ Bring in pets. Make sure they have a two-week supply of food. Make sure they are wearing identification.

❏ To sterilize the bathtub, scrub with household soap, swab with bleach, rinse thoroughly, let dry. Seal the drain with a silicone caulk that you can easily remove later. Fill the tub with water.

❏ Put valuables and documents in waterproof containers.

❏ Stock your safe place with a first-aid kit, small supply of food and water, flashlight, games for the kids, blankets and a mattress.

❏ Review with family members escape routes out of the house.

❏ Make sure everyone knows where the fire extinguisher is.

❏ Stay indoors unless you absolutely must go out. ■

JOE RAEDLE

Shoppers at a grocery store in Fort Lauderdale gather provisions in anticipation of Andrew.

FOODSTUFFS

It's time to top off your supplies.

❏ Apples, lemons, bananas, oranges. All will keep several days at room temperature.

❏ Individual servings of pudding.

❏ Individual servings of applesauce.

❏ Individual servings of diced fruit.

❏ Individually packaged juices and drinks.

❏ Raisins, dried fruits.

❏ Nuts.

❏ Cheese spreads and cheese slices that don't need refrigeration.

❏ Gum, hard candy.

❏ Ready-made baby formula, not the powder or concentrate.

❏ Baby food.

❏ Cookies.

❏ Crackers and chips.

❏ Dry cereal. Get the small boxes.

❏ Bread, muffins, bagels.

❏ Summer sausage, pepperoni.

❏ Condiments, including ketchup, mustard, onions, garlic, oil and vinegar.

❏ Canned vegetables.

❏ Bottled water, unless you have plenty.

❏ Ice.

❏ If you have not yet bought canned goods or other staple items, buy them now. ■

BATTEN DOWN

Protect yourself — secure the outside of your house.

Things to do outside as the storm approaches:

❏ Close shutters, lash down awnings or mount plywood over your windows and sliding glass doors.

❏ Identify locations of water, gas and electric shut-offs. You should shut them off if you have to evacuate.

❏ Bring in anything that could blow around: toys, bicycles, garbage cans, patio furniture, gas grills, etc.

❏ Lower your TV antenna, but first unplug the television. And be careful not to touch power lines with the antenna.

❏ Don't drain the swimming pool. The lack of water increases chances of the pool popping out of the ground. Add extra chlorine to the pool to reduce contamination. Do not sink lawn furniture into the pool; you could ruin the pool's surfacing.

❏ Turn off power to the swimming pool pump, pool lights and chlorinator. If the pool pump is exposed, wrap with a waterproof cover and tie it securely.

❏ Clean out gutters and downspouts.

❏ Lash trash containers together and then to a pole.

❏ Take down trellises.

❏ Forget about trimming the trees; no one will come to pick up the debris at this point, and the storm could turn your trimmings into airborne missiles. ■

THE ASSOCIATED PRESS

A worker tapes a window at a **South Carolina hotel as Hugo bears down in 1989. Shutters are much better.**

JOE RAEDLE

As Andrew approaches, Ralph and Sam Cohn put up shutters at their shop along State Road A1A in Fort Lauderdale.

■ TELLING THE CHILDREN

As a storm approaches, children's fears can intensify. Grown-ups can help calm fears with a common-sense, parent-to-kid talk.

You should start talking with your children about the coming storm, and what you're going to do about it, 24 to 36 hours before it arrives.

Before talking to your children, however, make sure you are calm enough not to frighten them.

"Do not, I repeat do not, talk to your children when you are still upset," says Veronica V. James, director of Family Services, Child Care Connection of Broward County. "It only makes the child upset."

Cassandra Walker, 8, still has nightmares about Andrew, which ruined her family's home. When frightening gusts returned during the Great Storm of '93, she screamed to her mother: "How come you lied to me? Andrew came back. Look he's here."

Parents should explain again that a hurricane is a giant windstorm, destructive and dangerous, but survivable with preparation and precaution. The more children know about the storm and safety procedures, the more confident they will be during the storm and recovery.

Remember that younger children may have trouble understanding the idea of a hurricane. Talk to them instead about its effects. They need to know that a hurricane can destroy homes and leave families without food, water and electricity.

Allow children to participate in the learning process. Ask your children to close their eyes and imagine pouring rain and the sounds of whipping wind. Tell them the wind might knock down trees and houses and overturn cars. Then tell them to imagine how dark it is when they sleep at night –

KIDS' PLAY
Gather up items to keep your children occupied.

Here's a checklist of things to do for children at home or in a shelter:

❏ Allow your children to help prepare for the hurricane. Give them a list of items to gather for the family's survival supplies.
❏ Allow them to prepare their own special supply kit, filled with goodies.
❏ At the grocery, allow children to pick out some of their favorite foods.
❏ If evacuating, let children pack a favorite game or toy. Make sure it's relatively quiet and doesn't take up much space.

A child's supply kit should be equipped with the same things included for an overnight stay at Grandma's.

❏ Games and toys.
❏ A favorite blanket or stuffed animal.
❏ Favorite books.
❏ Favorite food.
❏ Toothbrush and toothpaste.
❏ Rain gear.
❏ Paper, pencils, coloring books and crayons.
❏ Flashlight, extra batteries.

During the storm:
❏ Children can listen to parents tell stories from their lives.
❏ Stories that call for participation, by clapping or repeating lines on cue, are best for relieving stress, especially for young children.
❏ Sing songs. Singing helps relieve stress. ■

and tell them that if winds knock out power, that is what it will be like.

Tell children the storm might be so strong that you won't be able to stay home. You might have to go to a relative's home, a hotel or a shelter — a place where other families will gather.

Make sure children understand how important it is for them to listen to adults during the storm.

Wherever you stay, children should be firmly warned to stay away from windows and doors. Explain that the storm might grow quiet during the passing of the hurricane's eye, but that the rain and roar will begin again after the eye has passed. The calm period can last 30 seconds to 30 minutes.

It's important for children to feel they are a part of the preparations. Allow them to help pack safety kits, which should include toys and games. ■

BOB MACK

As Anna Garcia rests at a shelter in Homestead, Florida, her daughters Georgina, left, and Ginette talk with kids who were displaced by Hugo in 1989. If you go, expect only basic accommodations.

helters are not hotels or friends' houses. They are typically schools that provide a large "safe" area inside a sturdy building. They tend to be barren. Most creature comforts are carried in by the visitor.

Information about which shelters are open in your area will be available through newspapers, television and radio. Be aware that shelter locations can change quickly, so stay informed.

Most public shelters are run by the Red Cross, but that does not mean medical care will be available.

Some shelters will have food, others will not. It is best to bring your own. And do not expect to find a bed.

Be ready to set up a home away from home on the floor if you did not bring chairs and bedding.

Hundreds of other people will be in the shelters, so be prepared to deal with a large cross-section of the community.

Go to a shelter as soon as an announcement is made that it is open; space is limited. Remember to secure your home and shut off water, gas and electricity before you leave. ■

SHELTER SUPPLIES
You'll have to bring basics as well as amenities.

❏ Flashlight with extra batteries.
❏ Radio with extra batteries.
❏ Medicine.
❏ Snacks for the first 24 hours.
❏ Baby food and diapers.
❏ Blankets or sleeping bags.
❏ Cot (optional).
❏ Pillows.
❏ Identification showing home address.
❏ Photocopies of valuable papers, such as insurance documents.

(The originals should be in a safe-deposit box.)
❏ Playing cards, games or books.
❏ Eyeglasses.
❏ Hearing aids.
❏ Dentures.
❏ Special-diet foods.
❏ Toiletries.
❏ First-aid kit.

What not to bring:
❏ Guns.
❏ Alcohol.
❏ Pets. ■

Broward County hurricane shelters

The list of shelters is subject to change. Call the Broward County Emergency Preparedness Office, 765-5020, or the Red Cross, 763-9900, to double-check the status of your designated shelter.

NORTH BROWARD

1. Coral Springs High School, 7201 W. Sample Road, Coral Springs
2. Forest Glen Middle School, 6400 Wiles Road, Coral Springs
3. Deerfield Beach High School, 910 SW 15th St., Deerfield Beach
4. Coconut Creek High School, 1400 NW 44th Ave., Coconut Creek
5. Ely High School, 1201 NW Sixth Ave., Pompano Beach
6. Pompano Beach Middle School, 310 NE Sixth St., Pompano Beach
7. J.P. Taravella High School, 10600 Riverside Drive, Coral Springs
8. Tamarac Elementary School, 7601 University Drive, Tamarac
9. Ramblewood Middle School, 8505 W. Atlantic Blvd., Coral Springs
10. Silver Lakes Middle School, 7600 Tam O'Shanter Blvd., North Lauderdale

CENTRAL BROWARD

11. Piper High School, 8000 NW 44th St., Sunrise
12. Boyd Anderson High School, 3050 NW 41st St., Lauderdale Lakes
13. Lauderdale Lakes Middle School, 3911 NW 30th Ave., Lauderdale Lakes
14. Dillard High School, 2501 NW 11th St., Fort Lauderdale
15. Castle Hills Elementary School, 2640 NW 46th Ave., Lauderhill
16. Lauderhill Middle School, 1901 NW 49th St., Lauderhill
17. Plantation High School, 6901 NW 16th St., Plantation
18. Lauderhill P.T. Elementary, 4747 NW 14th St., Lauderhill
19. Bair Middle School, 9100 NW 21st Manor, Sunrise
20. Plantation Middle School, 6600 W. Sunrise Blvd., Plantation
21. Seminole Middle School, 6200 SW 16th St., Plantation
22. South Plantation High School, 1300 Paladin Way, Plantation

SOURCE: American Red Cross

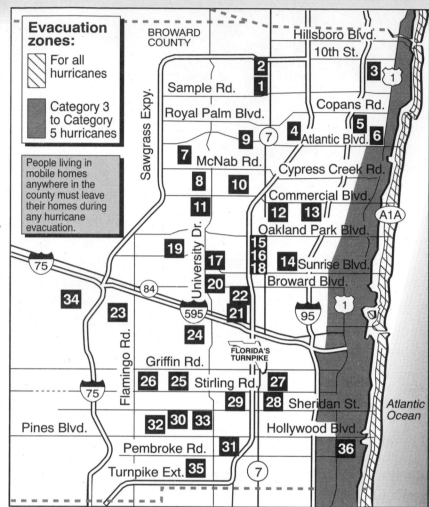

Evacuation zones:

▨ For all hurricanes

▨ Category 3 to Category 5 hurricanes

People living in mobile homes anywhere in the county must leave their homes during any hurricane evacuation.

SOUTH BROWARD

23. Western High School, 1200 SW 136th Ave., Davie
24. Cooper City Elementary School, 5080 SW 92nd Ave., Cooper City
25. Pioneer Middle School, 5350 SW 90th Ave., Cooper City
26. Griffin Elementary, 5050 SW 116th Ave., Cooper City
27. Hollywood Hills High School, 5400 Stirling Road, Hollywood
28. Sheridan Hills Elementary, 5001 Thomas St., Hollywood
29. Sheridan Park Elementary, 2310 N. 70th Terr., Hollywood
30. Pembroke Lakes Elementary, 11251 Taft St., Pembroke Pines
31. Pembroke Pines Elementary, 6700 SW Ninth St., Pembroke Pines
32. Pine Lakes Elementary, 10300 Johnson St., Pembroke Pines
33. Pasadena Lakes Elementary, 8801 Pasadena Blvd., Pembroke Pines
34. Tequesta Trace Middle School, 1800 Indian Trace, Weston
35. Miramar High School, 3601 SW 89th Ave., Miramar/Pembroke Pines
36. Hallandale High School, 720 NW Ninth Ave., Hallandale

Palm Beach County hurricane shelters

The list of shelters is subject to change. Call the Palm Beach County Emergency Management Office, 233-3500, or the Red Cross, 833-7711, to double-check the status of your designated shelter.

NORTH AREA

Jupiter to Riviera Beach
1. William Dwyer High School, 13601 N. Military Trail, Palm Beach Gardens
2. Palm Beach Gardens High School, 4245 Holly Dr., Palm Beach Gardens
3. Watson B. Duncan Middle School, 5150 117th Ct. North, Palm Beach Gardens

CENTRAL AREA

West Palm Beach to Lantana
4. West Palm Beach Auditorium, Palm Beach Lakes Boulevard and Congress Avenue, West Palm Beach
5. Palm Beach Lakes Community High School, 3505 Shiloh Drive, West Palm Beach
6. Lake Worth Middle School, 1300 Barnett Drive, Lake Worth
7. Santaluces High School, 6880 Lawrence Road, Lantana
8. Crestwood Middle School, 64 Sparrow Road, Royal Palm Beach
9. Wellington High School, 2101 Greenview Shores Blvd., West Palm Beach
10. Wellington Landings Middle School, 1100 Aero Club Dr., West Palm Beach
11. Palm Beach Community College, 4200 S. Congress Ave., Lake Worth
12. Conniston Middle School, 673 Conniston Rd., West Palm Beach
13. Bear Lakes Middle School, 3505 Shenandoah Blvd., West Palm Beach

SOUTH AREA

Boynton Beach, Delray Beach, Boca Raton
14. Christa McAuliffe Middle School, 6500 Lechalet Blvd., Boynton Beach
15. Atlantic High School, 2501 Seacrest Blvd., Delray Beach
16. Bibletown Community Church, 601 NW Fourth Ave., Boca Raton
17. Spanish River High School, 5100 NW Yamato Road, Boca Raton
18. Olympic High School, 20101 Lyons Road, Boca Raton
19. Florida Atlantic University, 500 NW 20th St., Boca Raton
20. Boca Raton High School, 1501 NW 15th Ct., Boca Raton
21. Omni Middle School, 5775 Jog Rd., Boca Raton
22. Pompey Park Recreation Center, 240 NW 10th Ave., Delray Beach

SOURCE: American Red Cross

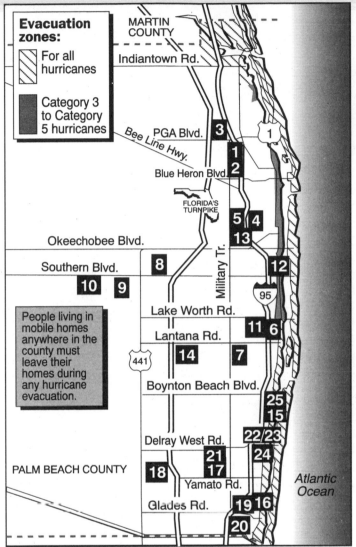

Evacuation zones:

For all hurricanes

Category 3 to Category 5 hurricanes

MARTIN COUNTY

Indiantown Rd.

Bee Line Hwy.

PGA Blvd.

Blue Heron Blvd.

FLORIDA'S TURNPIKE

Okeechobee Blvd.

Southern Blvd.

Military Tr.

95

Lake Worth Rd.

Lantana Rd.

441

Boynton Beach Blvd.

Delray West Rd.

Yamato Rd.

Glades Rd.

PALM BEACH COUNTY

Atlantic Ocean

People living in mobile homes anywhere in the county must leave their homes during any hurricane evacuation.

23. Delray Beach Civic Center, 50 NW First Ave., Delray Beach
24. Carver Middle School, 301 SW 14th Ave., Delray Beach
25. Boynton Beach Civic Center, 128 E. Ocean Ave., Boynton Beach

WEST AREA

Belle Glade, Pahokee, South Bay (not shown on map)
- Glades Central High School, 425 W. Canal St., Belle Glade
- Pahokee High School, 900 Larrimore Road, Pahokee
- Palm Beach Community College (West), 1977 College Dr., Belle Glade
- Lake Shore Middle School, 1101 SW Ave. "E", Belle Glade

Dade County evacuation zones

Because Dade County's list of shelters changes so frequently the county does not release shelter lists until a storm is threatening. But you should not wait that long. Call the county at 596-8735 or the Red Cross at 326-8888 to find out what the four or five nearest shelters are to you.

Evacuation zones:

For all hurricanes	Category 2 or greater hurricanes	Category 3 to Category 5 hurricanes

People living in mobile homes anywhere in the county must leave their homes during any hurricane evacuation.

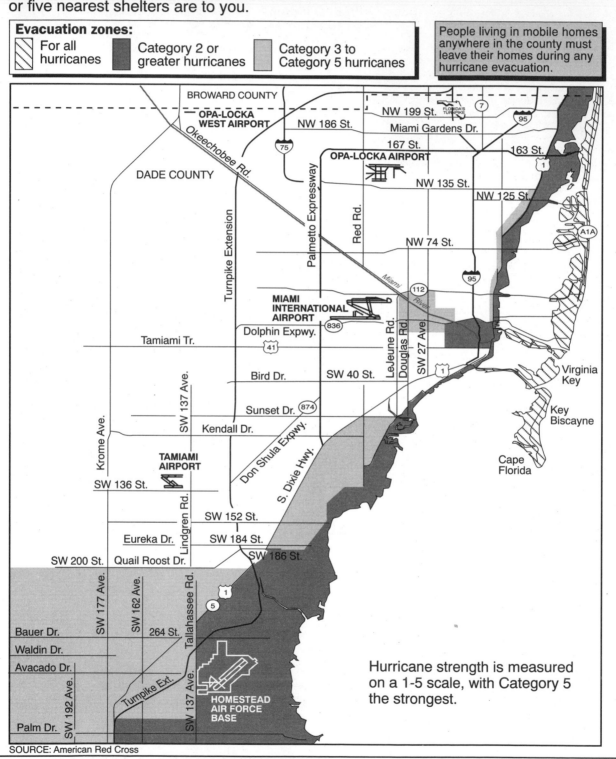

Hurricane strength is measured on a 1-5 scale, with Category 5 the strongest.

SOURCE: American Red Cross

Monroe County shelters and evacuation plans

The Keys, because of their unique geography, must be evacuated early and quickly. There are two evacuation plans — one for weaker hurricanes, another for major hurricanes. No matter the strength of the hurricane, it's best to get out early.

■ **For Category 1 and 2 hurricanes**, anyone who lives in a low-lying area, directly adjacent to the water, or in a mobile home should go to shelters in the Keys indicated by zones on the map below. But those shelters fill up quickly. And the shelters can change throughout the year. Call **1-800-427-8340** or **305-289-6018** to double-check on shelter availibility. Residents who are sick, elderly, disabled or at least six months pregnant — and people staying in state parks, camps and RV parks — should follow instructions, below, for stronger storms and evacuate to the mainland.

■ **Everyone in the Keys must evacuate when Category 3, 4 or 5 hurricanes threaten.** When you leave the Keys, go to Florida International University, the designated shelter in Dade County for Monroe County residents. Take the Florida Turnpike Extension north from Florida City to the FIU exit at U.S. 41/SW Eighth Street. Because of traffic jams and concerns that people will be stuck on the road, Keys officials will stop the evacuation at a certain time in certain places before the storm hits and tell stragglers to hunker down as best they can.

ZONE 1 - KEY WEST
Key West north to Shark Key Bridge.

1. Glynn Archer Elementary School
   1302 White St., Key West

2. Scottish Rite Temple
   533 Eaton St., Key West

ZONE 2 - LOWER KEYS
Shark Key Bridge to Seven Mile Bridge.

1. Sugarloaf Elementary School
   Upper Sugarloaf Key (MM 19, bay side)
   One block north of US 1 on Crane Blvd.

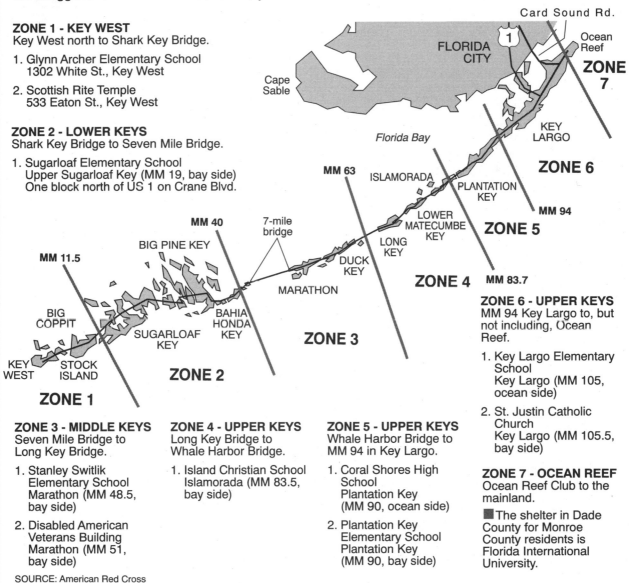

ZONE 3 - MIDDLE KEYS
Seven Mile Bridge to
Long Key Bridge.

1. Stanley Switlik
   Elementary School
   Marathon (MM 48.5,
   bay side)

2. Disabled American
   Veterans Building
   Marathon (MM 51,
   bay side)

SOURCE: American Red Cross

ZONE 4 - UPPER KEYS
Long Key Bridge to
Whale Harbor Bridge.

1. Island Christian School
   Islamorada (MM 83.5,
   bay side)

ZONE 5 - UPPER KEYS
Whale Harbor Bridge to
MM 94 in Key Largo.

1. Coral Shores High
   School
   Plantation Key
   (MM 90, ocean side)

2. Plantation Key
   Elementary School
   Plantation Key
   (MM 90, bay side)

ZONE 6 - UPPER KEYS
MM 94 Key Largo to, but
not including, Ocean
Reef.

1. Key Largo Elementary
   School
   Key Largo (MM 105,
   ocean side)

2. St. Justin Catholic
   Church
   Key Largo (MM 105.5,
   bay side)

ZONE 7 - OCEAN REEF
Ocean Reef Club to the
mainland.

■ The shelter in Dade
County for Monroe
County residents is
Florida International
University.

■ EVACUATION TIPS

I t's time to get in your car and go.

Long before this storm threatened, you, like thousands of South Floridians who stayed during Andrew, decided you would not stick around next time.

This is next time.

First, a reality check for those who made the easy passage from South Florida to points north during Andrew: This time, travel will be much more difficult. ·

A lot more people will be joining you. North-south roads will be crowded.

Remember: Fleeing may increase your chances of surviving the storm, but it will not guarantee it. Wherever you are, it will be scary, uncomfortable and dangerous.

If you still want to go, here are some tips:

■ Finish battening down your home. The best way to protect your abode — whether you're staying or going — is to put up shutters, or plywood or metal window covers.

■ Move patio furniture, hanging plants and gas grills inside. If your home is likely to sustain damage from rising water, raise valuables and expensive furniture as best you can.

■ Confirm reservations if you plan to stay at a motel.

■ Notify your relatives or friends to expect you.

■ Know of other places between your home and ultimate destination where you could stay if roads are clogged and you can't return home. Make a list of telephone numbers for all those places.

■ Before you leave, turn off electricity at the main circuit breaker or fuse box. That will protect your appliances from power surges and reduce the risk of your getting electrocuted by live, dangling wires after the hurricane. If you don't know

TIM RIVERS

Interstate 95 traffic heads north through Palm Beach County, away from the approaching Andrew. Next hurricane, even more residents are likely to flee.

where the circuit breakers are, unplug your appliances.

■ If your house is supplied with natural or propane gas, turn it off at the meter or tank.

■ Make a final walk-through inspection of your home just before you close the door. Look for valuables that you need — keys, checkbook, credit cards.

When Hurricane Gloria was headed toward Morehead City, North Carolina, in 1985, police went door to door dropping off "Stupid Forms" for those who chose to stay. The last item asked for those who stayed to name their next of kin.

■ Make sure you have packed your car wisely. Include a first-aid kit, water and food, dry clothes, flares, and extra gasoline in approved containers.

■ Don't try to tow a trailer or boat in high winds. It is too hazardous.

■ It is possible that traffic will be so congested near home that you'll realize you can't get anywhere. If so, go back home.

■ Don't ride out a hurricane in your car alongside the road. Know where emergency shelters are along the route you plan to take. ■

PET PRINCIPLES

Your animal's safety, well-being depend on you.

Here's what to do with your pet when the storm is threatening:

At home

❑ Make sure the pet has plenty of food and water.
❑ Make sure the pet is wearing a collar with identification.
❑ Try to make the pet as comfortable as possible; give it a safe, familiar place to stay and leave a familiar towel or blanket.

Taking your pet

❑ Call ahead to hotels and motels to make sure they allow pets.
❑ Use a portable carrier or cage to travel with household pets. The carrier should be large enough for the animal to stand up and turn around in.
❑ If you travel with the pet, bring along a collar with identification, a familiar towel or blanket, a supply of water and food, a leash and any needed medications.

Boarding

❑ Make early arrangements to leave the pet in a kennel or private clinic or with friends or relatives.
❑ Use a portable carrier to move the pet.
❑ Make sure the animal is wearing identification.
❑ Provide a familiar towel or blanket, a supply of water and food, a leash and any needed medications.

Leaving the pet

❑ Leave your pet alone only as a last resort. Do not let your pet roam. This would violate county ordinances.
❑ Bring the pet inside, away from the dangers of wind, water and debris. Keep in mind that storm noise can frighten animals.
❑ Stock up on newspapers, paper towels, trash bags and cat litter.
❑ Keep a pet first-aid kit on hand, with salve and bandages.
❑ Leave the pet with enough food and water for at least five days. Water should be the priority; a pet in good health can survive several days without food. Fill the bathtub or a nonspill container with water.
❑ Do not leave vitamins or mineral supplements where the pet can get to them; overeating such things can poison an animal.
❑ Leave a soft towel or blanket for the animal to rest on.
❑ Choose an enclosed garage, utility room, or bathroom, preferably with a tile floor to make cleanup easier. The room used should be a place the animal has lived in before, and ideally should not have any windows.

Exotic pets

❑ Remove the pet from the home even if you don't plan to leave; take it to a friend's unthreatened home or a pet shelter. Exotic pets such as parrots, reptiles or ferrets usually require specialized care and feeding and are more sensitive to environmental changes than dogs or cats.
❑ The pet should be transported in a roomy container or crate.
❑ Exotic pets usually eat special foods and may not eat substitutes. Keep a 7-to-10 day supply of food and water to take with the animal.
❑ If you leave the pet, place it in a nonglass, wire or mesh container. Place it high enough where flooding will not drown it.

Livestock

❑ Make sure livestock animals have a license or ID tag.
❑ Some animal control officials believe livestock are better off in a pasture. Others recommend sheltering them in a stable, barn or shed.
❑ Provide a seven-day supply of water and food. ■

A pony turns away from the wind as Hurricane Allen nears the Texas Gulf Coast in 1980. Whether you've got a dog or cat, an exotic pet or livestock, you should know what to do with your animal during a hurricane.

NICHOLAS R. VON STADEN

Hours after Andrew passed, a man in a dinghy in Highland Beach, Florida, about 80 miles north of the center of the storm's wrath, braves strong winds to check lines tying off boats in a canal off the Intracoastal Waterway.

Hurricane watch flags are flying. It's time to employ the plan for your boat that you worked out before storm season started.

The rush starts when actual hurricane warnings are issued. That's when flotilla plans, designed to move the largest number of boats in the shortest period of time, are invoked to coordinate the opening and closing of drawbridges with boat traffic.

If you're going to join a flotilla or head inland, make sure your ship is in shape to move by checking the fuel, fuel filters, batteries and bilges.

Emergency authorities will announce over radio and television when the flotilla plan will be invoked. Within a few hours, draw bridges will be locked in the down position.

However, no rule says you can't get started now.

If you're going to stay at the marina, or dock inland, tie down the vessel properly. Do not

■ BOAT PLANS IN ACTION

impede boat traffic by anchoring in the middle of the canal or river.

If you have chosen to remove your boat from the water and take it home by trailer, do it now to save time. Waiting will mean lines at boat ramps.

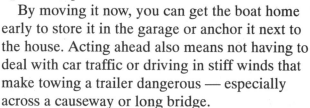

By moving it now, you can get the boat home early to store it in the garage or anchor it next to the house. Acting ahead also means not having to deal with car traffic or driving in stiff winds that make towing a trailer dangerous — especially across a causeway or long bridge.

Whether you tie down at a marina, a private dock or in your yard, remove all canvas and other features that could catch the wind. Also, remember to remove the radio and other easily salvageable items.

Above all, remember that no boat is worth your life. ■

Protecting your boat in a hurricane

Whatever preparations you must make for your boat, make them early.

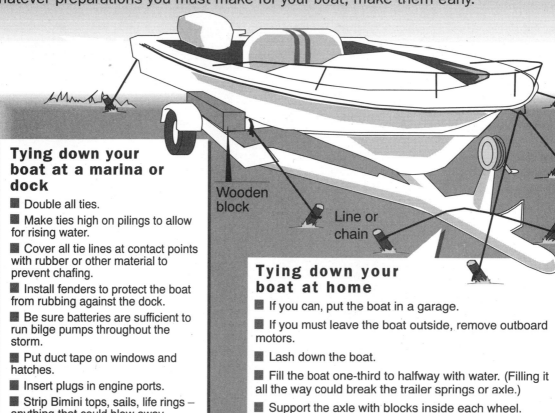

Wooden
block

Line or
chain

Tying down your boat at a marina or dock

■ Double all ties.

■ Make ties high on pilings to allow for rising water.

■ Cover all tie lines at contact points with rubber or other material to prevent chafing.

■ Install fenders to protect the boat from rubbing against the dock.

■ Be sure batteries are sufficient to run bilge pumps throughout the storm.

■ Put duct tape on windows and hatches.

■ Insert plugs in engine ports.

■ Strip Bimini tops, sails, life rings – anything that could blow away.

■ Disconnect shore power.

■ Close fuel valves, and cockpit seacocks.

Tying down your boat at home

■ If you can, put the boat in a garage.

■ If you must leave the boat outside, remove outboard motors.

■ Lash down the boat.

■ Fill the boat one-third to halfway with water. (Filling it all the way could break the trailer springs or axle.)

■ Support the axle with blocks inside each wheel.

■ Remove any item that could blow off the boat.

■ Place the boat away from trees or objects that could fall on it.

Finding safe harbor

■ If the boat cannot be removed from the water, it should be sailed to a safe refuge and secured there to ride out the storm.

■ Many marinas must be evacuated during a hurricane alert. Check your dockage lease and consult the dockmaster.

■ Canals leading inland offer varying degrees of protection for boats, but with the exception of the New River in Fort Lauderdale, all major east-west waterways are blocked at some point by floodgates, limiting their usefulness.

■ Consult the dockmaster and fellow boaters for suggestions.

■ Drawbridges limit movement of large vessels, and ground traffic will get priority in an evacuation. Boat owners should act ahead of an evacuation order.

■ If you decide to move your boat inland, make a test run to ensure the water is deep enough and overhead clearances are high enough.

Emergency phone numbers

Coast Guard

Broward County	305-927-1611
Palm Beach County	407-844-4470
Dade County	305-536-5641
Monroe County: Upper Keys	305-664-4404
Middle Keys	305-743-6778
Lower Keys	305-292-8800

Florida Marine Patrol

Broward County	305-467-4541
Palm Beach County	407-624-6935
Dade County	305-325-3346
Monroe County	305-289-2320

In October 1989 in Galveston, Texas, Wilfred Kildodeaux, right, helps retrieve a car that washed off a sea wall into the Gulf of Mexico. Try to avoid being stuck in your car during a hurricane — the results could be disastrous.

THE ASSOCIATED PRESS

CAR AND DRIVER

The storm's coming — take care of your vehicle.

Fill the tank with gasoline. Check oil, water levels.

❏ Store your automobile in a garage or carport.

❏ If you are in a flood-prone area, move your car to higher ground.

❏ If you must leave your car outdoors, park next to a building, away from trees or poles that may topple onto it.

❏ Make sure your vehicle has an emergency first-aid and tool kit.

❏ Stay out of your car during a hurricane.

❏ If you are unexpectedly told to evacuate, know that you are likely to encounter heavy thunderstorms and flooding.

❏ Listen to the radio for instructions. Never drive around barriers. ∎

PLANE PROBLEMS

If flying away is too risky, tie down your aircraft.

The skies may soon be too unfriendly for you to fly away from the storm. Unless you've already made arrangements, there may not be room in a hangar.

❏ If you're going to fly your plane to safety, make sure you'll have enough time to return home to board up the house and care for the family.

❏ Or you could deal with the house and family first, then try to fly out before it gets too windy. But that can be dangerous, particularly for newer pilots.

❏ As a last resort: Tie down the plane. Follow the basic procedure in the plane's manual. Small aircraft generally have three built-in loops. Use rope to tie those loops firmly to the runway.

❏ Be warned: Tying down the plane may not do much good. ∎

Chapter 5

IN THE STORM

The winds are picking up, the storm is making landfall. The moment of truth has arrived. You can't do much now except hunker down.

Stay indoors. Stay sober. Get everyone into your "safe place" before the storm hits. Bring in your food, water, first-aid supplies and portable radio or television.

Bring in a mattress to cover yourself with in case debris starts flying. Turn off electricity if flooding begins. Use flashlights, not candles.

"What do you do? You just sit there and sweat it out," says Arthur St. Amand, Broward County's director of Emergency Preparedness.

If you were in an evacuation zone and did not leave when you were told, you still have a chance to do so.

Officials don't advertise this because they want everyone in an evacuation zone to leave, but they do have a recommendation for stragglers. It's called last-resort refuge.

They recommend that as a last resort you go to a two-story or taller building. If you choose a high-rise, avoid the upper

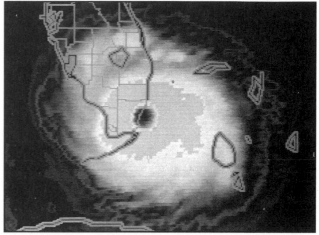

WTVJ-CH. 4

A computer-enhanced satellite image shows Andrew, the third-strongest hurricane to hit the U.S. this century, shortly after landfall in south Dade County.

floors, where winds are strongest, and the ground floor, where flooding could be a problem. Within that building find a parking garage or an interior room, preferably with no windows and on the second or third floor. Protect yourself as best you can, say, by taking cover under a mattress.

Don't go outside if it suddenly becomes calm. The storm's eye may be passing, and the eye is followed by the most vicious part of the storm.

Don't go outside until government officials give the "all clear" signal through the media. ■

September 1926: The view south on Andrews Avenue, a main road in Fort Lauderdale, shows the street clear of debris a few days after the hurricane. The damage, however, would take months to repair. After hitting South Florida, the Category 4 storm traveled into Alabama.

FORT LAUDERDALE HISTORICAL SOCIETY

VOICES OF EXPERIENCE

"I was holding onto the roof and calling to my mother. … I'd say, 'Mama, are you there?' and she'd answer, until after a while, she didn't answer anymore."

HURRICANE OF 1926

Virginia Shuman Young was 9 years old and her family had been in Fort Lauderdale only five months when the hurricane struck.

The sky grew red, the winds howled and water gushed into her home on Southeast Ninth Street. The house flooded, and the family's furniture began to bob like corks on the ocean.

Virginia's mother, a 6-week-old baby in her arms, climbed atop a tall wardrobe. Virginia and her other two siblings stood on chairs and tables.

"At the time we thought it was fun. We really didn't know what was happening," says Young, a former Fort Lauderdale mayor.

Her father, a sea captain, removed a closet door from the hinges and nailed a dresser drawer to it so the drawer would float. He lined the drawer with rubber sheeting and placed the baby inside.

Virginia and her siblings changed into swim-suits. Her father tied a rope around the waists of the children, then attached the rope to the closet door knob. He gave each child a tablespoon of whiskey.

"He kept us calm," Young says. "He did the best he could. Pretty good, I would say — we all made it through."

The hurricane hit South Florida on September 18, then traveled across the Florida peninsula and into Alabama. In all, 243 people were killed.

HURRICANE OF 1928

Helen McCormick remembers the unnamed hurricane for the night 17 members of her family died.

Her mother's instructions had been firm: They would ride out the storm in the house. So McCormick's family — 19 people in all — gathered at her stepfather's home in Chosen, a small settlement just north of Belle Glade.

About 9 p.m., McCormick, 13 at the time, saw a huge gush of water pouring into town. As the water rose to as high as 6 feet, someone carved an escape hatch in the house's roof. A piano became the ladder to climb to the hatch.

"I was holding onto the roof and calling to my mother. First me, then my brother," McCormick says. "I'd say, 'Mama, are you there?' and she'd answer, until after a while, she didn't answer anymore."

The flood uprooted the house.

"I thought it would beat me to death," McCormick says of the flood.

Of her family, only McCormick and her stepfather survived this country's second-deadliest hurricane. The storm killed 1,836 when it struck Lake Okeechobee and the surrounding area on September 16.

◼

What many Lake Okeechobee-area survivors remember most about the 1928 hurricane were the bodies the storm left behind.

"Bodies were stacked like cordwood," Carmen Salvatore says. "Piled up like cordwood at the Pahokee dock. No caskets that I remember, just bodies."

HURRICANE CAMILLE, 1969

Val Husley sat on the edge of his bed waiting for Camille.

He was too tired to move, too scared to sleep.

In the hours before Camille's deadly landing at Biloxi, Mississippi, Husley, then 28, boarded up his and other townfolks' homes. Using half-inch plywood, they made makeshift hurricane shutters.

"We knew something bad was coming," Husley recalls. "We knew it would be beyond anything we could imagine.

"When I walked outside the next morning, the most striking thing I saw was the trees. They were nude. Stripped naked by the wind and looking like skeletons," Husley says.

On his way to check on his grandparents, Husley saw homes that had been lifted from their foundations. He saw wood-frame houses reduced to mountains of sticks. Water was everywhere, soaking everything.

Husley's grandparents survived. So did his family and close friends. Husley is now curator of a hurricane museum in Biloxi.

Camille hit the Mississippi/Louisiana coast on August 17. It then crossed through Tennessee, Kentucky, West Virginia and Virginia, killing 256 people in all.

HURRICANE HUGO, 1989

George A. Fletcher remembers Lincoln High School as the shelter that became a hostage of nature, a hostage of Hugo.

LAWRENCE E. WILL MUSEUM, Belle Glade, Florida

September 1928: Belle Glade, Florida, on Lake Okeechobee, was devastated by a hurricane. The death toll: 1,836.

JOHN CURRY

September 1989: A weary Ann Ingle, left, pauses as family members and friends clean up her devastated home near the ocean in Surfside, South Carolina, after Hurricane Hugo smashed into it. Ingle says she moved to South Carolina from Delray Beach, Florida, because she felt too vulnerable to hurricanes there.

It was in that McClellanville, South Carolina, school that Fletcher, 66 at the time, and hundreds of others nearly drowned as the killer storm bashed the coast. The school was a public shelter, but residents soon learned it was much too low to withstand floods spawned by Hugo.

"When we looked through a door and saw the water rising in the hallways, we realized how intense the situation had gotten," says Fletcher, a retired Presbyterian minister. "We all felt like we were going to drown. People started screaming.

"We began standing on tables. But we needed to get the children up much higher. So we pushed the ceiling in."

The adults formed a line and passed the children hand-to-hand up to the air-conditioning ducts where they were told to stay.

"That's when it really got wild. The kids were scared and wanted to come back down into their parents' arms, but we couldn't let them. We were trying to save the poor little things."

The water suddenly receded and the worst was over. The group trudged to the gym where everyone sat in silent darkness until Hugo had

THE ASSOCIATED PRESS

September 1989: Residents of Charleston, South Carolina, begin clearing debris and trying to salvage items from their destroyed homes the day after Hurricane Hugo ravaged the coast.

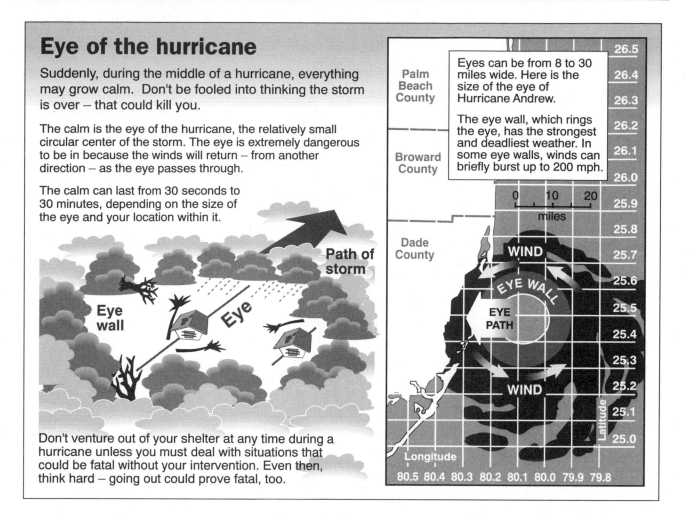

Eye of the hurricane

Suddenly, during the middle of a hurricane, everything may grow calm. Don't be fooled into thinking the storm is over – that could kill you.

The calm is the eye of the hurricane, the relatively small circular center of the storm. The eye is extremely dangerous to be in because the winds will return – from another direction – as the eye passes through.

The calm can last from 30 seconds to 30 minutes, depending on the size of the eye and your location within it.

Path of storm

Eye wall

Eye

Don't venture out of your shelter at any time during a hurricane unless you must deal with situations that could be fatal without your intervention. Even then, think hard – going out could prove fatal, too.

Palm Beach County

Broward County

Dade County

Eyes can be from 8 to 30 miles wide. Here is the size of the eye of Hurricane Andrew.

The eye wall, which rings the eye, has the strongest and deadliest weather. In some eye walls, winds can briefly burst up to 200 mph.

0 10 20 miles

WIND

EYE WALL

EYE PATH

WIND

Latitude

Longitude

80.5 80.4 80.3 80.2 80.1 80.0 79.9 79.8

26.5 26.4 26.3 26.2 26.1 26.0 25.9 25.8 25.7 25.6 25.5 25.4 25.3 25.2 25.1 25.0

---

run out of steam.

"The most horrible thing about that night was the thought that everyone in that building could have perished," Fletcher says.

Hugo pounded South Carolina on September 21, days after hitting Puerto Rico and the Virgin Islands. The death toll: 27.

■

A newspaper clipping on a wall at the National Hurricane Center details the fate of each of the 26 people killed in South Carolina during Hurricane Hugo in 1989.

Some drowned because they did not fear storm surge enough to evacuate. Some burned to death because they were using candles, which touched off fires, instead of using flashlights. Some were crushed in the mobile homes they had been told to flee.

Below the clipping, center Director Robert Sheets has placed a small note: "Most of these deaths could have been prevented."

■

"I drove back to my home from Charlotte. I parked about two miles from my home and walked in. When I get to my driveway, I start to recognize clothing up in the trees hanging from the branches. I get closer to the house and see photographs, records, toys and more clothes scattered.

"My advice: When the evacuation is ordered, get your photographs and records and go. You can replace sofas and curtains. You can't replace photographs."

— Randy McClure, of McClellanville, about 35 miles north of Charleston, South Carolina., where Hugo hit.

CARL SEIBERT

August 1992: A man, upper left, searches for anything that can be salvaged from the wreckage of what was his mobile home near Tamiami Airport in south Dade County.

HURRICANE ANDREW, 1992

At 3:30 a.m. Monday, Joe McCarthy was sitting in his mother's house on Southwest 141st Street in Kendall, a neighborhood outside Miami. He was calm, but that would soon change.

The French doors were wiggling. A yellow rectangular sign bumped against the house. Ironically, the sign read: "No Outlet." No way out of Andrew's path.

McCarthy, 29 at the time, and his mother and sister scurried through the home, seeking safety. His mother and sister made it to a back bedroom, but McCarthy got trapped in the kitchen doorway.

Windows on the sides of the house blew out, and wind whooshed in.

McCarthy watched his furniture play musical chairs, watched bric-a-brac fly into the air.

The walls began to dance. Parts of the roof blew off.

McCarthy struggled to his sister and mother. The three pushed their way to another bedroom, where they spent the night huddled together, separated from the storm by only a double mattress.

"As we were preparing Sunday, it was a per-sonal kind of thing," McCarthy says about the day before Andrew struck. "Like, 'That storm is not going to come in and damage this place.' But now you realize there's nothing you can do — no matter how hard you try."

Andrew hit South Florida on August 24, and Louisiana on August 26. In all, 56 people died.

■

Andrew simplified Mike Staats' life.

The Air Force pilot who used to fly F-16s out of Homestead Air Force Base says the storm stripped away his concern for the unimportant.

"Since Andrew, you wake up and concern yourself only with your daily activities — where you will get a meal, where you will find gas, where you will take your next cold shower."

■

"I think I called God over 100,000 times."
— Mercedes Figuera, who stayed in her mobile home at Honey Hill Mobile Park Home in Carol City, Florida, during Andrew. ■

Chapter 6

PICKING UP THE PIECES

The storm is over. The worst is not. More people die after a hurricane than during. There may be no more wind or high water, but hazards still abound. A wrong step could be fatal.

Downed power lines may still be live. If you touch one, you won't be.

Gas lines may be leaking. A spark from a cigarette or an electrical switch could trigger an explosion.

Broken glass can shred feet, especially children's. Nails and other sharp debris are everywhere.

Snakes and other dangerous critters may be lurking.

Your water is probably tainted.

If your house has not fallen apart yet, it may still do so — with you in it.

Looters may be down the street.

On top of all that, you and your neighbors have just gone through the scare of your lives. You would like to think it's all over, but the work facing you seems overwhelming.

"The storm is bad enough," says Arthur St. Amand, the Broward Emergency Preparedness director. "The recovery is long term. It's agonizing."

Now, more than at any time in your

JIM VIRGA

Leo Daykin, amid the wreckage of his trailer in Homestead, Florida, searches for mementos.

life, you need government help. It probably won't be there for a few days, at best.

You are on your own, like the only doctor in a busy emergency room. Set priorities and tackle the life-threatening situations before you handle the small things.

Six hours of living hell are over. Up to six months of working like hell are about to begin. Take your time. Do not overexert yourself. People need you. ■

AFTER THE STORM

Here's what to do — and what not to do — first:

Stop, don't move. There are all sorts of hazards around. Don't get hurt.

❏ Check your family and neighbors. Treat injuries with your first-aid kit. Try to call for help if injuries are beyond your expertise to treat.

❏ Call police or utility companies immediately to report any sparking or downed power lines. Stay away from trees touching power lines. Stay out of puddles. Don't bother now to report interruption in electric, gas, water or telephone service. Report individual problems with your utility service only after neighborhood service has been restored.

❏ Don't touch any electrical appliances, wires or equipment unless they're in a dry area or you're standing on a dry piece of wood while wearing rubber gloves and rubber footwear. Don't turn on anything electrical until an electrician can check the house.

❏ Don't strike matches until you're sure no gas is leaking.

❏ Be careful of sharp objects. Wear heavy boots and gloves when working in debris. There probably will be lots of broken glass around.

❏ Don't use the water until the local water utility, through the media, says it's safe to do so. Use only bottled or disinfected water.

❏ Monitor the storm and government officials on radio or television. Pay attention to emergency workers.

❏ Notify one out-of-town friend or family member that you are safe and ask that person to tell everyone else. Otherwise, stay off the phone; it's needed for emergency workers.

❏ Make temporary repairs necessary to stop further losses from the elements or looters. Keep receipts.

❏ Be aware that walls and ceilings may have been weakened and could fall at any time.

❏ Open all windows to air out the house.

❏ Do an inventory of your supplies. How much food is left? How much water?

❏ Check food for spoilage. Don't open the freezer, refrigerator or ice chest often.

❏ Get insurance documents and other important papers.

❏ Find the closest place to get relief or help.

❏ Beware of snakes, insects and frightened animals that may take up lodging in your home.

❏ Avoid driving. Roads may be littered with tire-damaging nails. Traffic lights may not be working and signs may be blown down, increasing the risk of accidents.

❏ When putting up a TV antenna, make sure it doesn't touch power lines.

❏ Don't overexert yourself.

❏ Obey all curfews. ∎

JOHN CURRY

Lynne and Jack Weis survey damage from a large pine that toppled onto their house. Beware: Touching a tree that's touching a power line could kill you.

WATER DO'S AND DON'TS

Boil-water orders aim to protect your health.

LOU TOMAN

T.J. Durand drops off a bottle of water for hurricane survivors at a pickup point in Fort Lauderdale.

Boil-water orders are often issued after a hurricane. That's usually because the public water utility has lost pressure in its water-moving systems, making it possible for contaminants to enter water lines. Pay attention to local authorities on the status of your water supply.

❏ Use only bottled or disinfected water for drinking and cooking until the public water supplies have been declared safe. The danger with tainted public supplies is from bacterial contamination that can cause severe diarrhea. Untreated diarrhea can be life-threatening.

❏ Water that you saved in bottles before the storm should be good for up to six months, if properly stored. Proper storage means leaving no air in the container and storing in the dark. When in doubt, disinfect it.

❏ Use disinfected or bottled water to brush your teeth and to give to pets.

❏ To prevent the spread of disease, wash your hands frequently with disinfected water and soap.

❏ Don't use water that has a dark color, an odor or contains floating material.

❏ Use water stored in the bathtub, from the pool or from the tap to flush the toilet. Don't drink or cook with water from the pool.

❏ Bathing or showering with tap water is fine, but don't let it get in your ears. And if you shave with tap water, dab any cuts with antiseptic.

❏ Don't drink water from wells, especially in areas of sewage contamination.

❏ Use bottled water for cleaning contact lenses.

Avoid most health problems by disinfecting any tap water you'll use for cooking or drinking. Always use clean containers. Here's how:

Boiling
❏ Boil at a rolling boil for 10 minutes.
❏ Let cool.

❏ Add a pinch of salt for taste.
❏ Pour the water back and forth between clean containers to reduce the flat taste.

Liquid chlorine
❏ Use common household chlorine bleach, without lemon scent.
❏ Follow the instructions on the label. If no instructions are available, add 8 drops of chlorine bleach to each gallon of water.
❏ Mix thoroughly.
❏ Let stand for 30 minutes.
❏ If water does not have a slight chlorine odor, repeat the dosage and let stand for 15 minutes.

Chlorine tablets
(can be obtained at drug stores or sporting goods stores) or iodine tablets

❏ Follow directions on the package. If directions are not available, use 1 tablet for each quart of water.
❏ Make sure the tablet dissolves; mix thoroughly.
❏ Let stand for 30 minutes.

Liquid iodine
(tincture of iodine)

❏ Add 5 drops of 2 percent United States Pharmacopie (USP) tincture of iodine to each quart of clear water.
❏ For cloudy water, add 10 drops of 2 percent iodine to each quart of water.
❏ Mix thoroughly.
❏ Let stand for 30 minutes. ■

AFTER-STORM COOKING

Choices are limited, but you've still got to eat.

When power goes out, choices for ways to cook dwindle. But alternate methods of heating are available, and some foods can be eaten cold.

Canned fuel, or Sterno, is sufficient to warm liquids. But it won't get a frying pan hot enough to cook a hamburger. Conventional gas grills, camping stoves and wood fires will provide enough heat to cook most foods.

❏ The first and most important rule is to cook outdoors only. Indoor grilling can cause a fire, release dangerous fumes or asphyxiate occupants of a house.

❏ Avoid cooking or preparing too much food; you don't want waste or leftovers. Eating unrefrigerated leftovers can lead to food poisoning.

❏ Dress up each meal with colorful paper plates, paprika or pimentos and hard candies for dessert. Little touches lift spirits.

Recipes for the grill

Tomato chicken

▲ Cut into quarters a 2 1/2 -to-3-pound broiler chicken.
▲ Place bone side down on grill over medium-hot coals for 20 to 30 minutes. Turn chicken and cook 30 to 40 minutes longer, turning frequently.
▲ Sprinkle with salt or pepper after chicken has browned. Top with tomato sauce made from crushed canned tomatoes and Italian spices.
▲ As an alternative to tomato sauce, brush the meat with soy sauce, bottled Italian dressing or lemon-pepper spices.

Chicken-chicken noodle

▲ Add a can of chicken meat to any chicken soup for a more hearty dish.
▲ A dash of garlic powder or pepper adds flavor.
▲ Heat in saucepan over grill.

More-than-stew

▲ Start with a can of beef stew.
▲ Add other canned vegetables — mushrooms, onions, peas, green beans or whatever you like.
▲ Heat in saucepan over grill.
▲ Of course, instead of beef stew, you can add canned vegetables to other canned soups.

Grilled steak

▲ Select a 1-inch thick steak, 1 pound per person, including bone.
▲ Trim most of the fat and slash remaining fat to prevent curling.
▲ Place steak on grill.
▲ Sprinkle with salt and pepper after turning and again after removing from grill.
▲ Cook 7 minutes for medium and 10 minutes for well done.

"Bostonish" baked beans

▲ 2 (1 pound) cans pork and beans
▲ 1/4 cup brown sugar
▲ 1 small chopped onion
▲ 3 tablespoons molasses
▲ 1 teaspoon salt
▲ 1/4 teaspoon dry mustard
▲ 1/8 teaspoon black pepper
 Mix ingredients and heat in a saucepan over grill.

Recipes requiring no heat

Three-bean dinner salad

▲ 2 (5-ounce) cans Vienna sausage
▲ 1 (16-ounce) can marinated bean salad with its dressing
▲ Cut sausage into 1/2-inch pieces. Combine with bean salad. Makes 2 servings.

Potato salad and sausage

▲ 1 (5-ounce) can Vienna sausage
▲ 1 (15 1/2-ounce) can heat-and-serve German potato salad
▲ Cut sausages into 1/2-inch pieces. Combine with potato salad. Makes 1 to 2 servings.

Turkey a la king

▲ 1 (18 1/2-ounce) can ready-to-serve cream of chicken soup. (This soup is not condensed; you don't need to add water.)

▲ 2 (5-ounce) cans white turkey in water, drained
▲ 1 (6-ounce) can sliced carrots or no-salt-added peas, drained
▲ 4 to 8 slices bread
▲ Combine soup, turkey and vegetables. Serve over bread slices. Makes 4 servings.

Corned beef hash supreme

▲ 1 (15 1/2-ounce) can corned beef hash, cut into 1/2-inch slices
▲ 1 (1-pound) can peas, drained
▲ Ketchup, to taste
▲ Use hash slices to cover the bottom of a shallow dish. Pour peas on top and squirt with ketchup. Makes 4 servings. ∎

FOOD SAFETY

Follow these guidelines to avoid getting sick.

Before you cook, assess the safety of your food. When in doubt, throw it out. The young and the elderly are at the greatest risk for food poisoning.

Frozen foods

Beef, veal, lamb, pork, poultry:
❏ If still partially frozen, you can refreeze.

❏ If thawed and held at room temperature for less than two hours, cook and serve, or cook and refreeze.

❏ If thawed and held at room temperature for more than two hours, discard.

Casseroles, stews, pies
❏ If the food is still partially frozen, cook and serve immediately or refreeze.

❏ If thawed and held at room temperature for less than two hours, cook or reheat thoroughly and serve immediately.

❏ If thawed and held at room temperature for more than two hours, discard.

Hard cheese, butter, margarine
❏ If still partially frozen or thawed, refreeze or refrigerate. (Hard cheese is a good choice to buy in preparation for a hurricane because of its longer shelf life and nutritional benefits.)

Commercially packaged vegetables, fruits and juices
❏ If ice crystals are still intact, refreeze, but there may be some loss in flavor and texture.

❏ If thawed and held at room temperature for less than two hours, cook and serve. Juices can be refrozen.

❏ If thawed and held at room temperature for more than two hours, discard if mold or yeast smell.

Foods containing dairy products
(primarily desserts)
❏ If the food is still partially frozen, cook and serve or refreeze.

❏ If thawed, discard.

Refrigerated foods
Food kept in an unopened refrigerator for 24 hours is still cold and remains safe.

Milk
❏ Discard if unrefrigerated for more than two hours.

Fresh eggs
❏ Safe unrefrigerated for five to seven days. Discard if shells are cracked or odor or discoloration is present.

Hard-boiled eggs
❏ Discard if held at room temperature for more than two hours.

Hard cheese, butter, margarine
❏ Safe unrefrigerated if well wrapped. Discard if mold or rancid odor develops.

Fruits and vegetables
❏ Safe as long as they look acceptable. Discard if mold or yeast smell develops.

Fresh meats
❏ Discard after two hours above room temperature.

Lunoh meats/hot dogs
❏ Discard after two hours at room temperature.

Opened mayonnaise
❏ Toss after two hours unrefrigerated because it is made with eggs. (Margarine is a better choice as a sandwich spread because of its longer shelf life.)

Canned goods
❏ Eat within two hours after opening can. Bulging, rusty cans need to be tossed. ■

LOU TOMAN

Rebecca Boothe stocks canned goods on a shelf at the south Dade home of Jean Letteriello, who had laid in a large food supply before Andrew hit.

HOUSE HINTS

Beware: Damaged homes pose dangers.

Getting your house back to normal can help you get back to normal.

But don't start working just yet. Take your time. Getting injured or making a bad decision out of haste will make a difficult situation worse. Regard your beloved home with a sense of mistrust.

"The inside of a damaged home poses all kinds of hazards," says Everett Rawlings, a builder and owner of a Boca Raton building inspection company.

❏ If your home looks unsafe, it probably is unsafe. Emergency-management officials have programs to certify structures for safety after a hurricane, and it is wise to wait for them.

❏ Assessing damage on your own requires the right gear, including dry, rubber-soled shoes; rubber gloves or work gloves; hammer; screwdriver; pencil and note paper.

❏ Protect your home from further damage by fixing roof leaks, or hiring someone to make emergency repairs. Use extreme caution if you plan to step onto the roof. Hurricane winds can weaken roof sheathing, and make the roof a dangerous place.

❏ Walk slowly around your home, looking for big problems such as whether your home shifted on its slab. Winds were so strong during Andrew that homes miles from devastated areas slid off foundations. Some roofs stayed intact but shifted. Such problems require professional repair.

❏ As you go inside, open all doors and windows to release moisture, odors and dangerous gases. If you cannot get a window open, use your tools to remove the sash. If a door won't open, remove the hinge pins and take off the entire door.

❏ Watch for dangers such as loose wires and sagging walls, roofs and ceilings. Be careful not to further weaken your home while removing debris.

❏ If the walls of a wood-frame home are waterlogged, drill or punch "weep holes" in interior walls to let water out and speed the drying process.

❏ If the walls don't appear to meet flush with floors and ceilings, inspect the slab below for damage.

❏ If you have wood floors that buckled, don't try to straighten them until they've dried. Then, take up the flooring and fasten it back down evenly. If you have ceramic or terrazzo tile on top of concrete flooring, let the floor dry, then reattach any loose tiles with appropriate cement or fastener. This job, too, may be best left to a professional.

❏ Brace walls where necessary with 2-by-4 studs.

❏ Remember, make only temporary repairs necessary to prevent further damage. Don't make permanent repairs until your insurance agent inspects the property. ■

SUSAN G. STOCKER

Jeff Pinder, right, and Eric Schinging, with hammer, put temporary roof on damaged home. Remember, hazards abound, so be careful during repairs.

CARL SEIBERT

Six months after Andrew, some Kendall, Florida, homes remain roofless; others have been repaired.

RATING THE ROOF

What to look for when making temporary repairs.

Do not inspect anything at night. Wait until daylight; use a good flashlight.

❏ Be careful when entering and moving around in a damaged home. If you smell gas, turn it off at the meter or tank. Do not smoke or use an open flame.

❏ Watch for loose electrical wires, and ceilings, beams and other objects that could fall. Never touch an electrical appliance or tool while standing in a wet area.

❏ Start in the attic, stepping only on wooden roof supports. If you step elsewhere, you could fall through the ceiling.

❏ Inspect roof supports, ridge areas, gable ends and eaves.

❏ While still inside, look skyward to detect holes where water can get in. Make note of those areas, so you know where to make exterior repairs.

❏ Use extreme caution — and wear rubber-soled shoes — if you decide to step onto the roof. Do not walk around; roofs that appear intact could have been weakened during a hurricane. You may want to use binoculars from the ground to hunt for damaged areas.

❏ Look for missing asphalt roof shingles and missing or broken roof tiles. On flat roofs, look for areas where the gravel surface and under-layment have been torn away.

❏ Remember to keep receipts for everything you buy; that will help ensure that your insurance claim gets paid.

❏ Emergency repairs can be made with self-adhesive roofing paper, which comes in rolls and has an adhesive side that sticks to the roof. Plastic sheeting, such as Visqueen, can also be used to stop leaks. Plastic sheeting should be at least 6 mils thick.

❏ Roofing paper is applied by alternating layers of trowel-grade roof cement and paper. Apply layers from the lowest part of the roof to the top.

❏ In the attic, broken roof supports can be repaired temporarily by running 8-foot (or longer) 2-by-4s on each side of a broken support, and nailing them to the broken support. ∎

Joan Poirier, Gregg Petronela and Suzanne Bedard huddle around a hurricane lamp after Andrew knocked out power. Using kerosene lamps or flashlights is advised. Candles are too dangerous.

JOHN CURRY

IN THE DARK

Tips for dealing with the loss of electricity.

Don't touch any electrical lines or equipment. Don't get on a ladder to take a closer look.

❏ Standing water anywhere near an electrical outlet is hazardous; so is water flowing through damaged walls. If there are any concerns that conditions are unsafe, call a licensed electrician.

❏ Treat all cables and wires as if they were electrically charged.

❏ The power company will restore power first to police and fire departments, hospitals, utility plants, Red Cross centers, government buildings and transportation centers.

❏ If everyone else in your neighborhood has power and you don't,

check all circuit breakers and fuses before calling the electric company.

❏ Turn off or unplug most electrical appliances (even if you have no power) so that power systems will not be overloaded when power is restored.

❏ Use flashlights or kerosene lamps. Candles are too dangerous.

❏ Before using a generator, read the instruction manual.

❏ Put the generator in a well-ventilated area.

❏ Appliances should be plugged directly into the generator. Don't overload the generator. Add up the wattage of each appliance and make sure the total is

Reconnecting power

■ Damage to the electrical conduit pipes above and below your electric meter, or to the metal box that holds the meter, will need to be repaired at your expense by an electrician.

■ The power company cannot restore power to your home until those repairs are made.

■ Damage to the meter itself, or to the power lines that feed your home's electrical service, are the power company's responsibility.

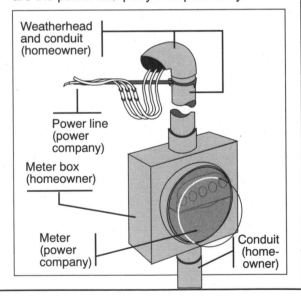

Weatherhead and conduit (homeowner)

Power line (power company)

Meter box (homeowner)

Meter (power company)

Conduit (homeowner)

lower than the wattage rating of the generator.

❏ Avoid connecting the generator to the home's main wiring at the breaker panel or fuse box; power

from the generator could surge back through power lines, posing a danger to personnel trying to make repairs. ■

AFTERMATH ESSENTIALS

Toilet flushing and garbage pickup pose challenges.

In most cases, you can still use your toilet after a storm. However, experts say you don't have to flush each time the toilet is used. Frequent flushing can overload already weakened electrical systems that power municipal and regional sewer systems.

❏ Remember the old rhyme used by various states during times of drought: "If it's yellow, let it mellow. If it's brown, flush it down."

❏ If no water flows into the bowl after flushing, you can still make the toilet flush by pouring about a gallon of water into the tank or bowl.

❏ If the toilet overflows, don't flush again until repairs can be made. Instead, experts advise that you get old-fashioned: Use a bucket. After the bucket is filled, it can be dumped into a portable toilet — usually set up at nearby shopping center parking lots.

❏ Never use the outdoors as a toilet. Even latrines are not advised. Health experts say that wastes left outside, even in treated latrines, contain bacteria that can taint water supplies and pose health risks if stepped on or touched.

Garbage

Garbage pickup, like everything else, will be slow immediately after a storm. If possible, call your local trash hauler to find out when service will be restored. In the meantime:

❏ Health officials suggest double-bagging all garbage in plastic bags. Keep the bags in covered containers. You can spray the inside of the containers with insect repellent.

❏ Don't pile trash next to utility poles or leave it in the street.

❏ If the smell becomes unbearable, find a neighbor with a pickup truck who can haul the garbage to a central collection point. Or, ask hurricane volunteers from outside the immediate area if they would take some trash back home. ■

Staying clean

A sun shower can help to get you clean after a day of toiling in the post-hurricane heat.

First, fill a large, strong plastic bag with water and hang it in the sun to get warm. You can buy a manufactured portable shower for $9 to $11 at camping supply stores, or you can use a sturdy plastic trash bag.

Inside, hang the bag of warmed water from your shower spigot. Outside, hang the bag from a tree in a private place.

With a manufactured shower, open the nozzle long enough for you to get wet, then close. Lather yourself with soap. Open the nozzle again and rinse.

If your shower is homemade from a trash bag, poke small holes in the bottom and stand underneath it.

Portable showers come in different sizes. A 4-gallon bag will provide two or three showers; a 5-gallon bag will give you three or four showers.

Staying cool

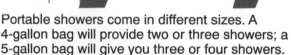

Here's what you can do to stay cool while rebuilding under the blazing Florida sun:

Wear loose, light-colored clothing and a hat.

Dampen yourself and your clothes. As the water evaporates, your skin cools.

Drink lots of liquids and eat small, light meals.

No alcohol – it raises your body temperature.

If possible, work in the shade.

Always wear a strong sunscreen.

Keeping cool at night:

Don't eat heavily or drink alcohol immediately before sleeping.

When sleeping outside, stay on the grass away from pavement, buildings and trees — they all radiate heat absorbed during the day.

Sleep on a woven mat or in a hammock instead of on a mattress to help air circulate under your body.

CLEANING HOUSE

Restore the condition of your personal effects.

Many insurance policies will cover the cost of professional cleanup if you cannot move a big mess yourself. Check your policy. If you must do it yourself, take "before" photos or videotapes.

Pump or bail water out of the house as soon as safely possible. Shovel mud out before it can dry. Open the windows to let the house air out and give the walls and floors a chance to dry. Scrub floors and walls with a stiff brush and mild soap and water.

Ovens
❑ Unplug as a safety precaution.

❑ Clean the outside thoroughly with a grease cutter, then with detergent and water.

❑ Clean the inside with conventional oven cleaner.

Refrigerators and freezers
❑ Unplug appliances as a safety precaution.

❑ To remove odors, wash the inside with detergent and water. Make sure you wash the plastic gasket that

seals the doors. Rinse with a cloth and clear water. Wipe dry.

❑ If odor remains, wash with a solution of 1 teaspoon of baking soda per quart of warm water. Or, you can use a cup of vinegar or ammonia to a gallon of water.

❑ If an odor is stubborn, spread about 3 ounces of powdered activated charcoal on a piece of aluminum foil or in a shallow pan. Put it on the refrigerator or freezer shelf. Foods can be stored with the charcoal.

❑ Keep the charcoal in the refrigerator until it becomes wet. Then, replace the charcoal. Repeat the process until the odor is gone. Keep all foods and beverages covered.

Washers, dryers, dishwashers
These appliances should be sanitized if they have been immersed in flood water. Here's how:

❑ Unplug the appliances as a safety precaution.

❑ Pour a disinfectant into the empty washer. Run a 15-minute cycle using the hot water

JIM VIRGA

Arturo Guzman salvages items from his demolished trailer in south Dade. Drawers from wet wood furniture should be pulled out to dry.

setting.

❑ Unplug the dryer and wipe the drum and dryer door with a cloth dipped in disinfectant solution. Rinse with a cloth dipped in clear water.

❑ Leave the dryer door open until all parts are dry — preferably overnight. When dry, the dryer can be used again.

❑ Leave the dishwasher door open until all parts are dry.

❑ Clothes baskets, work surfaces and containers where clothes will be placed also should be sanitized.

Clothing
Do not immerse flood-soiled clothing in hot, soapy water. If flood waters carried red or yellow clay, the hot soapsuds will set rust-colored stains. Here are the procedures for cleaning flood-soaked clothing.

Washables
❑ Brush off loose dirt and rinse several times to remove as much mud as possible.

❑ Machine wash clothes when no more dirt can be rinsed out.

❑ It will be necessary to sanitize  clothes because flood water may be contaminated with sewage. There are four types of disinfectants that can be used, depending on the type of fabric.

Disinfectants

❏ Disinfectants such as Roccal or Zephrin are safe for all fibers, including wool or silk, but may cause color changes. These disinfectants should be added at the beginning of the rinse cycle. For top-loading washers, add 4 tablespoons of Roccal or 2 tablespoons of Zephrin. For front-loading washers, use 2 tablespoons of Roccal or 1 tablespoon of Zephrin. These products are available in drugstores and dairy or janitorial supply houses.

❏ Liquid chlorine bleaches (such as Clorox or Purex) are safe for all fibers except wool, silk and water-repellent fabrics. Add bleach to wash water before putting clothes in machine, or dilute bleach in 1 quart of water before adding it to the wash cycle. Do not use bleach in the rinse cycle. Use 1 cup in top-loading washers and $1/2$ cup in front-loading washers.

❏ Pine oil disinfectants (such as Fyne Pine, King Pine, Pine-o-Pine or Texize-o-Pine) are safe for washables, except wool and silk. Make sure the product contains at least 80 percent pine oil. Add at the beginning of the wash cycle, preferably before putting clothes into the washer. Dilute in 1 quart of water

JUDY SLOAN REICH

Johnny Passmore Jr. shovels debris from his parents' south Dade home. Try to rid your home of water and mud as soon as possible so the home can dry.

before adding it to the machine. Use $3/4$ cup in top-loading washers and $1/2$ cup in front-loading washers.

❏ Phenolic disinfectants (such as Pine-Sol, Al Pine or Sea-Air) are safe for washables, except wool and silk. Use 1 cup in top-loading machines and $1/2$ cup plus 2 tablespoons in front-loading washers. Add these disinfectants to the wash or rinse cycle.

Mildew

❏ If mildew stains remain after washing with detergent and water, wash with a solution of 1 tablespoon bleach to a pint of lukewarm water. Before bleaching, spot-test colored garments.

Dry cleaning

❏ Let garment dry slowly at room temperature. Shake and brush well to remove dirt.

❏ Tell the cleaner the cause of stains and the fiber content, if possible.

Mattresses and pillows

❏ Flood-soiled mattresses should be sent to a commercial renovating company. Even after renovation, flood odor may not completely leave. It may be cheaper to buy a new mattress.

❏ If you decide to keep your mattress, it should be sterilized at a mattress company.

❏ Feather pillows, if the ticking is in good shape, can be washed. Brush off surface dirt. To let water circulate through, open a few inches of the seam on opposite cor-

ners of the pillow. Turn edges, sew loosely with a strong thread or fasten with safety pins. Wash in machine or by hand in warm suds 15 to 20 minutes. Use a disinfectant in the wash cycle. Do not wash more than two pillows at a time if using an automatic washer. Rinse at least three times in clear, warm water. Spin off water or gently squeeze out as much water as possible. Dry in an automatic dryer at moderate heat with several bath towels to speed drying. Or, dry in a warm room with a fan or put across two or three clothes lines.

Foam pillows

❏ Remove cover, brush off surface dirt. If no manufacturer's instructions are available, soak in cool water, then wash in warm suds by hand.

63

Rinse in lukewarm water. Squeeze out excess water. Dry away from heat or sunlight.

Wooden furniture

❏ Move wooden furniture outdoors and take out as many drawers or working parts as possible. Do not force stuck drawers with a screwdriver or chisel; remove the back and push out the drawers. Clean away all dirt and mud. Return the furniture indoors so it will dry slowly.

❏ To remove white spots, rub a turpentine-wrung cloth over furniture. Dry immediately with a cloth. Polish.

Upholstered furniture

❏ It may be impossible to salvage water-soaked furniture. If a piece seems to be worth the effort, you'll have to clean and oil the springs, replace the stuffing and clean the frame.

Books and papers

❏ Place books on end with leaves separated. When they are partially dry, pile and press books.

❏ Alternate drying and pressing until thoroughly dry.

❏ If books and papers are very damp, sprinkle cornstarch or talcum powder between the leaves to absorb moisture. Leave on for several hours, then brush off.

❏ When papers and books are almost dry, use an electric iron on low heat on the pages.

Separate the pages to prevent musty odors.

❏ When books are completely dry, close them and use C-clamps to help them retain their shape.

❏ Photocopy any very important papers

ELIOT J. SCHECHTER

Letica Paz, an Andrew victim, washes clothes the old-fashioned way — by hand, in a tub. Flood-soaked clothes may also need to be disinfected.

because they may quickly disintegrate, even though they've dried out.

Televisions, VCRs and stereos

❏ Never open an electronic appliance to dry it inside. A television is especially dangerous. It has a tube that retains electric voltage.

❏ Unplug the appliance and let it dry thoroughly. After moisture on the outside has dried, plug it in. If you see smoke or hear crackling sounds, unplug the appliance and take it to a repair shop.

❏ If the power indicator lights come on, leave the appliance on for about 10 minutes, then turn it off for about 30 minutes. Repeat the process, leaving the appliance on for an extra five minutes.

❏ VCRs often have moisture sensors that refuse to let the machine play a tape until dry. Don't despair yet; keep following the procedures above.

❏ If the appliance does not come on, unplug it and take it to a repair shop.

Rugs and carpets

❏ After shampooing, dry rugs or carpets quickly. Hang rugs on a line if possible, or lay them out flat in a warm, dry place. Use an electric fan to speed drying.

❏ Even though the surface seems dry, any moisture remaining at the base of the fiber tufts will cause mildew or rot.

❏ If you must walk on the carpet before it is dry, cover it first with brown paper towels. Vacuum again when dry and brush the nap in one direction. ■

JIM VIRGA

The Giffens — Dorothy, left, daughter Tamra and granddaughter Catlin — lost mobile homes to Andrew. Such a loss can trigger emotional stress months after the initial trauma. Children may be especially hard-hit.

The hurricane is gone. But if your psyche seems to be as much in need of repair as your shredded home, you've got emotional stress. Stress, no less than the storm and its destruction, can be difficult to deal with.

"After a disaster, people's lives have been turned upside down and they have no control," says Jane Morgan, the American Red Cross' associate for Disaster Mental Health Services in Alexandria, Virginia. "So the feelings of anger and disbelief are not unusual."

The signs of post-hurricane trauma are not always immediate; the emotional effects may not appear for months. Recovery time varies as well.

"Often the signs are there, but we are too busy to see them, too busy taking care of our house and family," Morgan says. "Sometimes we don't want to see them."

Stress takes its toll not only on those hit directly by the storm, but also on those who made it through physically unscathed. Mental health experts say the unscathed often suffer "survivor's guilt."

"They're very thankful they survived, but they

■ DEALING WITH STRESS

have a hard time enjoying the normal things of life," says Michael Culotti, a trauma specialist who worked with hurricane victims as a consultant for NationsBank. "One person said, 'How can I enjoy a chocolate chip cookie when I know people in south Dade don't have a roof over their head?'"

People suffering survivor's guilt often push themselves to the limit trying to help.

Children, in particular, resent the shattering of their routine. That resentment may manifest itself in enormous guilt, nightmares, temper tantrums and problems at school.

"Children tend to associate trauma with themselves," Morgan said. "They think, 'I had a fight with my mommy or I didn't make up my bed and look what happened.'"

The key to dealing with trauma after the storm is to understand that there is a natural grieving process — denial, questioning, acceptance and recovery — after the loss of normalcy, loved ones and property. ■

Filing a claim

There's more than one way to file an insurance claim.

In some cases, the process is "paperless" and all you need to do is call an agent.

In other cases, even after a phone call, you may be asked to fill out or sign a variety of forms. An "ACORD" form is a standardized property loss notice that asks for basic information such as name, address, policy number, mortgage company and a brief description of the damage.

Many insurers require you to fill out a "personal property inventory form," or "PPI," for claims on the contents of your home. The form is essentially a grid on which you itemize possessions lost.

PPI forms include the following instructions:

■ Separate damaged from undamaged items.

■ Use a separate form for each room of your home.

■ List the "replacement cost" of an item and its "actual cash value." **Replacement cost** is what it would cost today to replace an item with another just like it. **Actual cash value** is what your item was really worth after deducting for depreciation and wear.

■ Attach any documentation you can (receipts, photographs, canceled checks, credit-card statements, warranty booklets) to show what an item was worth.

Example PPI form

Item No./Quantity	Description of property	Mfr/Brand Name and Serial/Model number	Purchased or obtained from	Docu-menta-tion*	Date of purchase or age	Replacement repair or restoration cost	Today's value/ Actual cash value
TO BE COMPLETED BY INSURED							
*A-Appraisal E-Estimate	B-Paid bill or receipt P-Photo	C-Canceled check CR-Credit card receipt	O-Other			TOTALS	

FILING INSURANCE CLAIMS

Your home is damaged.
Here's what to do.

Try to call your agent immediately. Most major insurers have toll-free numbers.

❏ Begin making temporary repairs to prevent further damage. Save all receipts.

❏ Do not attempt to make permanent repairs on your home until an adjuster has inspected it.

❏ Most homeowners policies provide for removal of trees or branches that have fallen on your home. They usually don't pay for removal of trees or debris that blew into your yard without damaging anything.

❏ If your home is uninhabitable or you move somewhere else temporarily, be sure to let your insurer know where you can be reached. Industry officials say the spray-painting of important information on homes after Andrew proved effective. Your name

and correct address should be sufficient for an adjuster to find your policy. Don't include your policy number — someone else may take advantage of that. Don't assume that adjusters will know what street they are on — street signs may have blown away. Include a phone number where you can be reached.

❏ Insurers usually send adjusters to the worst-hit homes first. If your home suffered only minor damage, be patient.

❏ Many adjusters and agents are authorized to issue checks on the spot to cover the cost of temporary housing.

❏ Get bids from several licensed contractors on repair jobs and present them to your adjuster. You should be free to pick the contractor of your choice, with the adjuster's consent. Some companies provide lists of recommended contractors.

❏ If you and your insurance company

JACKIE BELL

Spray-painting your name and address on your damaged home is a good way to let the adjuster know you need service. Don't include your policy number.

can't settle on how much it will cost to repair your home, the Insurance Information Institute suggests contacting the company's claims department manager. If you still can't agree, you and the insurance company can present the claim to a state-run mediation program.

❏ Litigation should be a last resort in settling a claim. Cases can cost thousands of dollars in legal fees and take years to resolve. ■

Phone numbers, some of which are activated only after a storm, for insurance questions:

• Florida Department of Insurance Consumer Helpline 1-800-342-2762
• Hurricane help line 1-800-528-7094
• Aetna 1-800-238-6225
• GEICO 1-800-841-3000
• Liberty Mutual 1-800-537-8676
• Nationwide 1-800-421-3535
• Progressive 1-800-274-4499
• Prudential 1-800-437-3535
• State Farm 1-800-326-2431
• Travelers 1-800-842-6516
• USAA 1-800-531-8111

TIM RIVERS

Kurt Mickle, a professional tree trimmer, saws a toppled seagrape in Lauderdale-by-the-Sea, Florida. Don't do this kind of dangerous work yourself — leave it to a pro.

WHO FIXES IT?

TV, power and garbage services will be disrupted.

After the storm, nothing will be normal. Expect power outages, fallen power lines and debris strewn about.

❑ Call the power company if there are lines down or sparking in your yard.

❑ If the rest of your neighborhood has power and you don't, first check circuit breakers and fuses, then call the power company. But don't expect immediate satisfaction; the power company will concentrate on restoring power to whole blocks.

❑ Pile debris as neatly as possible and as close to the street as you can. Keep debris from cluttering utility poles. Crews will not be able to make repairs if their path is impeded.

❑ Garbage pickup will be delayed. Call your local trash hauler to find out when pickup will resume. Meanwhile, double-bag all garbage in plastic bags. Keep the bags in covered containers. Spray the inside of the containers with insect repellent.

❑ Your cable TV service will be out as long as you have no power. If cable service is not restored once power is restored, call your cable company. ■

Chain saw safety

Chain saws are handy – and dangerous. Make sure you follow the extensive safety instructions in the chain saw manual.

■ Work in an area free of obstructions. Avoid other branches and rocks. Make sure your clothing can't get caught in the chain saw. Be especially careful that you don't cut your feet.

Wear safety gear:

■ Keep children and spectators at least 30 feet away.

■ Never operate a chain saw from a ladder or tree.

■ Begin and continue cutting at full throttle.

■ Cut one log at a time.

■ Keep the chain properly lubricated. Fill the oil tank each time you refill the fuel tank. Clean the cooling system after every other refueling.

Position your body to the left of the cut and away from the saw chain when the engine is running.

Be particularly aware of a chain saw's potential for kickback, which can throw the saw's cutting edge back into your face or body.

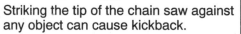

Striking the tip of the chain saw against any object can cause kickback.

Use two or more cuts on logs larger than the saw's cutting length.

Start cuts with the base of the chain. Pivot the blade at the base to work the blade through the wood. Never pivot on the tip of the saw.

■ Do not use the saw in bad weather.

■ Stop the engine before setting down the saw.

■ Don't walk with the saw running.

Storm-damaged landscaping

Take the cost of lost landscaping into account when making insurance claims or taking losses on income tax.

Be prepared for difficulties in finding replacement landscaping. Shortages of planting materials can exist for several weeks after a storm.

Here are some tips for helping your trees and plants spring back:

■ If more than one-third of a plant is missing, it may be quicker and less costly to replace it.

■ If the bark has been split and a significant portion of the cambium is exposed, the plant probably will not survive.

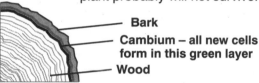

Bark

Cambium – all new cells form in this green layer

Wood

Uprooted plants and trees that have intact root balls can be replanted.

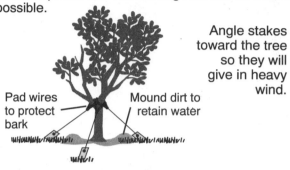

■ Cover exposed roots with wet towels or dirt until you can right the plant. Don't use plastic.

■ Restake plants that are leaning and trim as little as possible.

Angle stakes toward the tree so they will give in heavy wind.

Pad wires to protect bark

Mound dirt to retain water

■ Place 3 to 4 inches of wet mulch or compost over and around the base of newly planted or replanted trees and shrubs. Water daily, but don't saturate – roots need air, too.

■ As a rule, don't fertilize right after a storm. The plant is readjusting, so wait until it has shown new growth.

POOL CLEANUP

Keep your pool free of mosquitoes.
Clear out debris.

After a hurricane, your swimming pool may be a haven for mosquitoes and a repository for debris. Here's how to remedy those problems:

❑ Remove all large objects. Then clean the pool thoroughly to prevent stains from smaller debris.

❑ If you removed the pool's filter motor before the hurricane, reinstall it now.

❑ If you wrapped the filter motor to waterproof it, remove the wrapping and check for flooding. If the motor is wet, you may need to call a repair service.

❑ Lower the water to normal level so it can be skimmed properly.

❑ Balance the pH, superchlorinate and run filter until clear. Keep the pool superchlorinated until you get the filters going again or until you can get a professional to come. ■

LOU TOMAN

A boat that had been docked behind a home in Key Biscayne, Florida, sits swamped in the home's pool. Not all large objects can be removed quickly.

Volunteers should coordinate their efforts with organized groups to avoid hindering relief plans.

NICHOLAS R. VON STADEN

HOW TO HELP
Know what's needed and what's not.

Hurricane victims will need help. But before you do anything, find out what is needed most. Read newspapers, watch television and listen to the radio.

Don't go traipsing off to volunteer in the disaster area unless you are with an organized group or volunteer organization.

Don't donate clothing and furniture. Those items, and dealing with them, only hinder relief workers' efforts to get food, water and medical supplies into the disaster area.

Items to donate
❏ Water, sealed and bottled

❏ Non-perishable food, canned goods, Gatorade, juice, powdered milk

❏ Fire extinguishers

❏ Can openers

❏ Tools, mops, rakes, cleaning supplies, bleach, detergent, lime, plastic trash bags, plastic wrap, shrink wrap, packing tape

❏ Insect repellent

❏ Charcoal or gas grills, Sterno stoves and fuel

❏ First-aid supplies

❏ Flashlights and batteries

❏ Baby supplies (food, formula, diapers, wipes, medications, powder)

❏ Personal hygiene products and feminine products

❏ Radios

❏ Ice, bagged, in semi-trailer loads

❏ Pet food

❏ Cots

❏ Trucks, drivers, refrigerated semitrailers, pallets

❏ Roofing materials for temporary repairs: plastic sheeting at least 6 mils thick, quarter-inch to half-inch plywood, nails, furring strips, 8-penny nails, claw hammers, wood ladders, nail aprons, handsaws, utility knives and gloves

❏ Residential building materials: lumber, sheetrock, 8-penny and 16-penny nails, plumbing supplies and fixtures, electrical supplies and fixtures

Items not needed
❏ Clothing

❏ Alcoholic beverages

❏ Perishable foods

❏ Furniture ■

■ HELPING OUT VICTIMS

Trom he first impulse for many people not directly affected by a hurricane is to try to help those who were.

It's a noble impulse, but don't give in to it right away.

"It's extremely dark in the areas that need help the most, there's no street signs," says Command Sgt. Maj. Robert Long of the 7th Battalion 9th Field Artillery of the U.S. Army Reserve. "It's easy to get lost and get flat tires."

Hurricane victims and emergency workers don't need gawkers rushing to the disaster area, clogging up streets and causing even more confusion.

Stay away unless you're truly willing to help — and until you know precisely what help is needed.

Volunteer to work with only an organized, carpooling group that has been assigned specific tasks. Dress appropriately — wear work boots, gloves, hat and sunscreen. Carry your own food and water.

Remember that one of the easiest ways to help is to write a check to an appropriate charity.

The call for help after a hurricane is not an invitation to send garage-sale junk to the needy, so put away the coats and furniture. Storm victims need more basic things, such as food, water and blankets. ■

ANDREW ROWE

Chris Wilenta shovels debris as part of a relief effort two weeks after Andrew ravaged south Dade County.

National Guard Sgt. Steven Malvita, right, and a paramedic and another guardsman arrest a looting suspect near Homestead, Florida. You may not have the authorities' help if looters come after your property. So be ready to protect yourself.

JOE RAEDLE

LOOK OUT FOR LOOTERS

If chaos reigns, prepare to defend yourself.

Looters are the ugly opportunists of a hurricane.

Police say merchandise-laden stores are looters' primary targets. But after those wares have been picked over or are secured by authorities, looters will turn to the wreckage of homes. Protect yourself and your property.

Police say that spray-painted messages such as "You loot, I shoot," were a deterrent during Andrew.

❏ Stay outside, especially at night. Criminals usually won't go inside a home that has someone stationed outside.

❏ If possible, keep your home well-lighted at night.

❏ Get a dog or put up signs to make looters  think you have a dog.

❏ Lock your house if you can, especially if you aren't staying there at night.

❏ Don't use tarpaulins to secure your property. Police found that tarps gave criminals a place to hide after Andrew.

❏ Guns are a deterrent against criminals, but remember they can be used against you. ■

BUYER BEWARE

Profiteers are out there — avoid being gouged.

Despite tougher laws passed after Andrew, profiteers are still sure to surface after the next hurricane.

❏ If you need something, first ask a friend or relative who lives outside the emergency area to deliver or ship it to you. This is especially helpful for big-ticket items, such as electrical generators. Delivery, though, may take days.

❏ You can try to bargain with gougers, but it won't be easy. People who load trucks with goods and drive to emergency areas do it to make money fast.

❏ Don't hire unlicensed roofers or contractors, or fly-by-night tree trimmers. Andrew taught many homeowners that unqualified repair crews do lousy work or sometimes no work at all.

❏ If you know gouging is occurring, report it to the state Attorney General's Office, Consumer Division. In South Florida, the number to call is: 305-985-4780. Post-Andrew gouging slowed after newspapers and TV stations began reporting the names of people accused of gouging. ■

GET READY —AGAIN

Chapter 7

UNITED PRESS INTERNATIONAL

Residents of Tallahassee, Florida, inspect damage done by a tree toppled by Elena in 1985.

The storm has hit. You're picking up the pieces of your life.

The last thing you want to think about is another hurricane, but ... that's exactly what may be heading your way. Right now.

It's not unheard of. In fact, hurricanes often strike twice in the same place in the span of only a few years.

Two hurricanes hit Florida in the same year in 1906, 1916, 1924, 1926, 1928, 1933, 1935, 1945, 1947, 1948, 1950, 1966 and 1985. Many of those pairs of storms struck within a month of each other.

In 1964, three storms hit Florida.

Storms can even hit the same small area again and again. In Guam, which is only 30 miles wide, three typhoons plowed through the island in 1992.

Two other typhoons, as hurricanes are called in that part of the world, skirted the island.

"You have to be aware: Two weeks later, here comes another one," says National Hurricane Center Director Robert Sheets.

One of the first jobs for government officials after Andrew hit in 1992 was to plan for another hurricane.

That's your job, too. ∎

73

Hurricane frequency per century

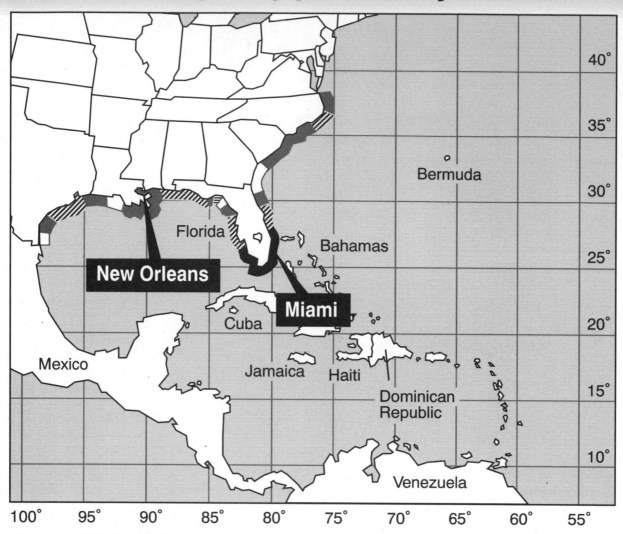

South Florida, on average, gets a hurricane every four years and a major hurricane — one with winds of at least 111 mph — every nine years.

Number of hurricanes with winds of 111 mph or higher that will hit land:

- 7 to 11 major storms a century
- 4 to 6 major storms a century
- 2 to 3 major storms a century
- 1 to 2 major storms a century
- 1 or fewer major storms a century

Hurricane strength is rated on a 1-5 scale, with Category 5 the strongest. Category 3 storms have winds of at least 111 mph, and are considered major hurricanes.

Deadliest hurricanes

Of the five deadliest storms to hit the United States in the 20th century, three hit South Florida or the Keys. None was named.

	Year	Category	Area hardest hit	Deaths
#1	1900	4	Galveston, Texas	6,000
#2	1928	4	Lake Okeechobee, Florida	1,836
#3	1919	4	Florida Keys, South Texas	600 to 900
#4	1938	3	New England	600
#5	1935	5	Florida Keys	408

Hurricane strength is rated on a 1-5 scale, with Category 5 the strongest.

Costliest hurricanes

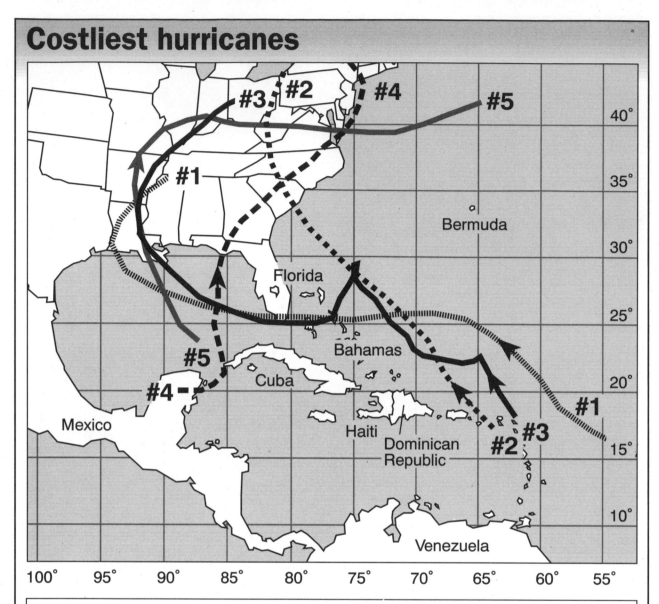

Of the five costliest hurricanes to hit the United States, two slammed South Florida. Damages are expressed in 1992 dollars:

	Name	Category	Year	Area hardest hit	Cost in billions
#1	Andrew	4	1992	South Florida, Louisiana	$20.0
#2	Hugo	4	1989	South Carolina	$7.91
#3	Betsy	3	1965	South Florida, Louisiana	$7.14
#4	Agnes	1	1972	Northeast U.S.	$7.1
#5	Camille	5	1969	Louisiana, Mississippi	$5.8

Hurricane strength is rated on a 1-5 scale, with Category 5 the strongest.

Strongest hurricanes

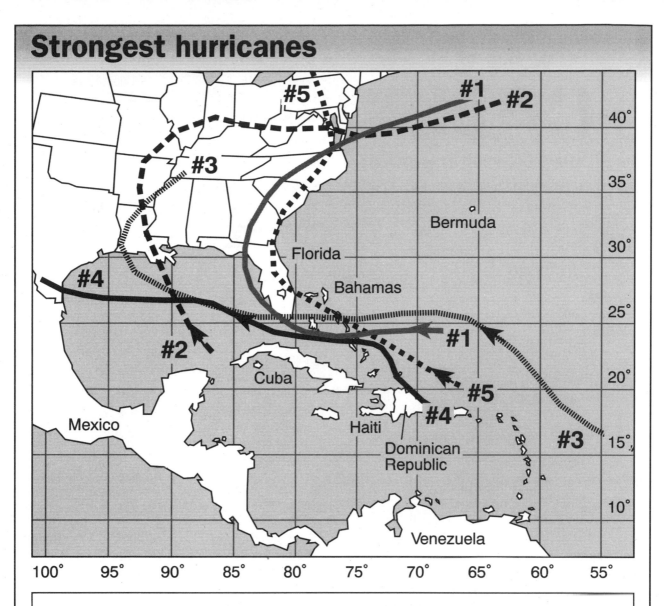

Of the five strongest storms to hit the United States, four landed in South Florida. The lower its barometric pressure, the stronger the storm.

	Name	Category	Year	Area hardest hit	Barometric pressure
#1	Unnamed	5	1935	Florida Keys	26.35
#2	Camille	5	1969	Louisiana, Mississippi	26.84
#3	Andrew	4	1992	South Florida, Louisiana	27.32
#4	Unnamed	4	1919	Florida Keys, South Texas	27.37
#5	Unnamed	4	1928	Lake Okeechobee, Florida	27.43

Hurricane strength is rated on a 1-5 scale, with Category 5 the strongest.

ON CALL

You'll need these numbers before and after the storm.

EMERGENCY 911

UTILITIES
Florida Power & Light
• Broward
305-797-5000
• Palm Beach County
407-395-8700
• Dade
305-442-8770
Florida Keys Electric Cooperative Association
• Monroe
305-852-2431
City Electric
• Key West
305-294-5272

Southern Bell
telephone repair 611

Gas companies
South Florida has hundreds of propane and natural gas companies. Consult your local phone directory.

EMERGENCY SHELTER, EVACUATION
Emergency Management Offices
• Broward
305-765-5020
• Palm Beach County
407-233-3500
• Dade
305-596-8700
— Hurricane hotline
305-596-8735

• Monroe
305-289-6018
1-800-427-8340

American Red Cross
• Broward County
305-763-9900
• Palm Beach County
407-833-7711
— Boca Raton
407-368-6622
• Dade County
305-326-8888
• Monroe County
305-852-9612
— Key West
305-296-3651

INSURANCE
Florida Department of Insurance
• Consumer Helpline
1-800-342-2762
• Hurricane help line
1-800-528-7094

Insurance companies
• Aetna
1-800-238-6225
• GEICO
1-800-841-3000
• Liberty Mutual
1-800-537-8676
• Nationwide
1-800-421-3535
• Progressive
1-800-274-4499
• Prudential
1-800-437-3535

• State Farm
1-800-326-2431
• Travelers
1-800-842-6516
• USAA
1-800-531-8111

PEOPLE WITH SPECIAL NEEDS

Area Agencies on Aging
• Broward County
305-485-6370
• Palm Beach County
407-837-5138
• Dade and Monroe
305-670-6500
(See also Emergency Management Offices)

Hearing-impaired
• Broward
305-357-5790
• Palm Beach County
407-233-3527
• Dade and Monroe
305-595-4749

Social Services Divisions
• Broward
305-357-6344
• Palm Beach County
— Delray
407-274-3130
— West Palm Beach
407-355-3030
— Riviera Beach
848-0601
— Jupiter
407-747-2007
— Belle Glade
407-996-1630
— Lake Worth
407-547-6834

• Dade
305-375-5656
• Monroe
— Upper Keys
305-852-7125
— Middle Keys
305-289-6016
— Key West
305-292-3515

MISSING CHILDREN
Missing Children Information Clearinghouse
1-800-342-0821

ANIMALS
Humane Society
• Broward
305-989-3977
or 305-463-4870
• Palm Beach County
407-686-3663
• Dade
305-696-0800
• Monroe
305-451-3848

Wildlife Care Center
• Fort Lauderdale
305-524-4302

STORM TRACKING, STORM NEWS
National Hurricane Center
Recorded information
305-662-5702

Newspapers
• Sun-Sentinel
— Fort Lauderdale
305-356-4500
— South Broward
305-436-7150

— West Broward
305-572-2000
— Palm Beach County
407-243-6600
• Diario Las Americas
305-635-3341
• El Heraldo de Broward
and Palm Beach
305-527-6659
• Key West Citizen
305-294-6641
• Miami Herald
– Dade
305-350-2111
– Broward
305-985-4525
• The News (Boca Raton)
407-395-8300
• Palm Beach Daily News
407-820-4770
• Palm Beach Post
407-820-4100

Television stations
• WPBT (PBS)
305-761-3516
• WTVJ (NBC)
305-525-3331
• WPTV (NBC)
— Palm Beach County
407-655-5455
— Broward
305-427-2283
• WCIX (CBS)
305-593-6606
• WSVN (Ind.)
305-524-0388
• WPLG (ABC)
1-800-950-9754
• WPEC (CBS)
1-800-273-9732
— Palm Beach County
407-844-1212

— Broward
305-427-0090
• WLRN (Edu.)
305-995-1717
• WAQ (Ind.)
407-688-0300
• WLTV (SIN)
305-471-3900
• WPBF (ABC)
407-694-2525
• WFLX (Fox)
407-845-2929
• WBFS (Ind.)
305-523-3333
• WTVX (Ind.)
407-686-3434
• WDZL (Ind.)
305-925-3939
• WXEL (PBS)
407-737-8000
• WHFT (Ind.)
305-962-1700
• WSCV (Ind.)
305-888-5151

AM radio
• 560 WQAM (B)
Talk/Sports
305-431-6200
• 610 WIOD (D)
Talk/Sports
305-759-4311
• 640 WLVJ (PB)
Religion/Talk
407-688-9585
• 710 WAQI (D)
Talk (Spanish)
305-445-4040
• 740 WSBR (PB)
Business Talk/Sports
407-997-0074
• 790 WMRZ (D)

SEAN DOUGHERTY

Hailed as a source of calm during the storm, TV weather forecaster Bryan Norcross helped thousands of frightened South Floridians get through Andrew.

Nostalgia Music
305-653-8811
• 850 WEAT (PB)
Easy Listening
407-965-5500
• 900 WSWN (PB)
Religion
407-996-2063
• 940 WINZ (D)
24-hour news
305-624-6101
• 980 WWNN (PB)
Motivational/Health Talk
407-997-0074
• 1040 WYFX (PB)
Urban Contemporary
407-737-1040
• 1080 WVCG (D)
Variety
305-445-1080
• 1140 WQBA (D)
News/Talk (Spanish)
305-447-1140
• 1170 WAVS (B)
Caribbean
305-584-1170
• 1220 WCMQ (D)
Latin Pop
305-854-1830
• 1230 WJNO (PB)

News/Talk
407-838-4300
• 1290 WBZT (PB)
News/Talk
407-965-9211
• 1320 WLQY (D)
Int'l Variety/News
305-891-1729
• 1340 WPBR (PB)
Nostalgia Music/Talk
407-582-7401
• 1360 WKAT (D)
Int'l Variety
305-949-9528
• 1380 WLVS (PB)
Religious
407-585-5533
• 1400 WFTL (B)
Talk
305-940-0755
• 1420 WDBF (PB)

Big Band
407-833-1420
• 1470 WRBD (B)
Urban Contemporary
305-731-4800
• 1490 WMBM (D)
Gospel
305-672-1100
• 1520 WEXY (B)
Religious
305-561-1520
• 1580 WSRF (B)
Album Rock
305-587-1035
• 1600 WPOM (PB)
Urban Contemporary
407-844-6200

FM radio
• 88.5 WKPX (B)
Alternative Rock
305-572-1321
• 88.9 WDNA (D)
Community Radio
305-662-8889
• 89.3 WRMB (PB)
Religious
407-737-9761
• 89.7 WMCU (D)
Religious
305-953-1155
• 90.3 WAFG (B)

Religious
305-776-7705
• 90.7 WXEL (PB)
Public Radio
407-737-8000
• 91.3 WLRN (D)
Public Radio
305-995-1717
• 92.3 WCMQ (D)
Latin Pop
305-854-1830
• 92.1 WRLX (PB)
Easy Listening
407-838-4306
• 92.7 WZZR (PB)
Rock
407-640-8410
• 93.1 WTMI (D)
Classical
305-856-9393
• 93.9 WLVE (D)
Jazz
305-654-9494
• 94.3 WOLL (PB)
Oldies
407-843-4616
• 94.9 WZTA (D)
Classic Rock
305-624-6101
• 95.5 WOVV (PB)
Contemporary
407-478-9688
• 96.5 WPOW (D)
Urban Contemporary
305-653-6796
• 97.3 WFLC (D)
Adult Contemporary
305-759-4317
• 97.9 WRMF (PB)
Adult Contemporary
407-838-4300
• 98.3 WRTO (D)
News/Tropical Pop
305-445-4040
• 98.7 WKGR (PB)
Classic Rock
407-686-9595
• 99.1 WEDR (D)
Urban Contemporary
305-623-7711

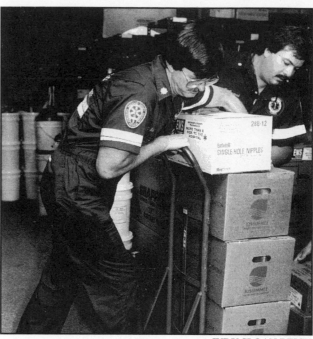

JUDY SLOAN REICH

Cmdr. Kenneth Scott, left, and Maj. Mike Haygood of Broward Emergency Medical Services prepare supplies for victims of Hugo in Puerto Rico in 1989.

• 99.5 WTRU (PB)
Latin Music (Spanish)
407-744-6398
• 99.9 WKIS (B)
Country
305-431-6200
• 100.7 WHYI (B)
Contemporary
305-463-9299
• 101.5 WLYF (D)
Adult Contemporary
305-653-8811
• 102.7 WMXJ (B)
Oldies
1-800-226-1027
• 103.5 WSHE (B)
Album Rock
305-587-1035
• 104.3 WEAT (PB)
Adult Contemporary
407-965-5500
• 105.1 WHQT (D)
Urban Contemporary
305-444-1880
• 105.9 WAXY (B)
Oldies

305-463-9299
• 106.7 WJQY (B)
Adult Contemporary
305-484-8107
• 107.5 WQBA (D)
Latin Pop
305-441-2073
• 107.9 WIRK (PB)
Country
407-965-9211

SOCIAL SERVICE
ORGANIZATIONS
American Red Cross
• Broward
305-763-9900
• Palm Beach County
407-833-7711
— Boca Raton
407-368-6622
• Dade and Monroe
305-326-8888

**Catholic Community
Services**
• Broward
305-522-2513

BOB MACK

Tourists lean into the wind as Floyd, barely strong enough to rank as a hurricane, skirts Key West in 1987.

• Palm Beach County
407-842-2406
 — south county
407-274-0801
• Dade and Monroe
305-754-2444

Crisis lines
• Broward
305-467-6333
• Palm Beach County
407-547-1000
 — south county
407-243-1000
 — Belle Glade
407-996-1121
• Dade
305-358-4357
• Monroe
305-296-4357

Jewish Federation
• Broward
305-748-8400
• Palm Beach County
407-478-0700
 — south county
407-852-3100
• Dade and Monroe
305-576-4000

**Mental Health
Association**
• Broward
305-733-3994
• Palm Beach County
407-832-3755

 — south county
407-276-3581
• Dade and Monroe
305-379-2673

Salvation Army
• Broward
305-524-6991
• Palm Beach County
407-295-9311
• Dade
305-643-4900
• Monroe
305-294-5611

United Way
• Broward
305-462-4850
• Palm Beach County
407-832-7300
 — south county
407-278-1323
• Dade
305-579-2200
• Monroe
305-296-3464

Urban League
• Broward
305-584-0777
• Palm Beach County
407-833-1461
 — south county
407-265-3318
• Dade and Monroe
305-696-4450

**Volunteer
Referral Service**
• Broward
305-522-6761
• Palm Beach County
407-881-9503
• Dade and Monroe
305-579-2300

GOVERNMENT LISTINGS

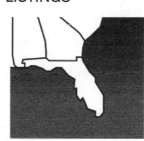

Florida
• Attorney General
Price gouging reports
305-985-4780
• Agriculture,
Department of
1-800-435-7352
• Child Abuse Hotline
1-800-962-2873
• Game and Fresh Water
Fish Commission
407-640-6100
 emergency
1-800-432-2046
• Health and
Rehabilitative Services

 — Broward
305-467-4352
 — Palm Beach County
407-837-5135
 — Dade
305-377-5000
 — Monroe
305-852-3243
• Highway Patrol
 — Broward
305-845-6000
 — Palm Beach County
407-588-8545
 — Dade
305-470-2500
 — Monroe
305-289-2300
• Insurance Commissioner
1-800-342-2762
• Consumer Assistance
 — Broward
305-467-4339
 — Palm Beach County
407-837-5045
 — Dade and Monroe
305-377-5235
 (See also Florida
Department of Insurance)

- Marine Patrol
  — Broward
  305-467-4541
  — Palm Beach County
  407-624-6935
  — Dade
  305-325-3346
  — Monroe
  305-289-2320

Broward County
(305-Area Code)
- Animal Control
  765-4700
- Aging, Area Agency on
  485-6370
- Building and permitting
  765-4927
- Bus information
  357-8400
- Cooperative
  Extension Service
  370-3725
- Emergency
  Services Division
  emergency 911
  non-emergency
  357-8248
- Emergency
  Preparedness
  disaster information
  765-5020

- Governmental Center
  357-7585
- Hotel & Motel Association
  462-0409
- Human Services
  357-6385
- Information,
  Broward County
  357-7585
- Medical Association
  739-2305
- Port Everglades
  523-3404
- Social Services Division
  357-6402
- Sheriff's Office
  emergency 911
  non-emergency
  765-4321
- Water and sewer
  765-4710

Palm Beach County
(407-Area Code)
- Administrative Complex
  — south county
  276-1225
- Aging and Adult Services
  930-5040
- Animal Control
  233-1200
  — south county
  276-1344
- Bus information, CoTran
  233-1111
  — south county
  272-6350
- Consumer Affairs
  355-2670
  — south county
  276-1270

- Cooperative Extension
  Service
  233-1700
  — south county
  276-1260
- Emergency Medical
  Services Division
  355-6050
- Emergency Management
  233-3500
  — south county
  276-1200
- Governmental Center,
  West Palm Beach
  355-3623
- Health Unit
  840-4500
  — south county
  274-3100
- Medical Society
  433-3966
  — south county
  276-3636
- Port of Palm Beach
  842-4201
- Public Safety
  355-4163
- Sheriff's Office
  emergency 911
  non-emergency
  688-3000
  — south county
  274-1075
- Water and utilities
  641-3429
  — south county
  278-5136

Dade County
(305-Area Code)
- Airport information
  876-7000

- Aging, Area Agency on
  670-6500
- Aging and Adult Services
  377-5068
- Animal Control
  884-1101
- Building and Zoning
  375-2500
- Citizen Services
  375-5656
- Cooperative
  Extension Service
  248-3311
- Emergency Management
  596-8700
- Fire Department
  emergency 911
  non-emergency
  446-7845
- Health Department
  325-2500
- Mosquito Control
  592-1186
- Police
  emergency 911
  non-emergency
  595-6263
- Public Works
  375-2730
- Rumor Control
  596-8735
- Sheriff's Office
  emergency 911
  non-emergency
  595-6263
- Social Services
  377-5068
- Street Maintenance
  — city of Miami
  575-5261
  — Metro-Dade
  592-3115
- Switchboard of Miami
  358-4357
- Water and
  Sewer Authority
  emergency
  274-9272

information
665-7471

Monroe County
(305-Area Code)
• Airport Information
296-5439
• Aging, Area Agency on
670-6500 (in Dade)
• Animal Control
— Upper Keys
451-0088
— Middle Keys
305-743-3779
— Key West
294-4857
• Ambulance
emergency 911
information
289-6004
• Building Department
852-1469
— Key West
294-4641
• Code Enforcement
289-6005
— Key West
292-4495
• Cooperative
Extension Service
— Upper Keys
852-1469 ext. 4501
— Middle Keys
743-0079 ext. 4501
— Key West
292-4501
• Emergency Management
289-6018 or
1-800-427-8340

• Emergency
Medical Services
emergency 911
non-emergency
289-6004
• Fire Department
emergency 911
information
289-6010
• Fire Marshal
289-6043
• Health Department
— Upper Keys
852-9216
— Middle Keys
289-2450
— Key West
292-6894
• Housing Authority
743-5765
— Key West
296-5621
• Poison Control Center
1-800-282-3171
• Mosquito Control
— Upper Keys
872-2573
— Middle Keys
743-6361
— Key West
296-2484
• Planning Department
— Upper Keys
852-7100
— Middle Keys
289-6031
— Key West
292-4491
• Public Safety Division
289-6002
• Public Works
— Upper Keys
852-7161
— Middle Keys
743-5632
— Key West
292-4560

• Sheriff's Office
emergency 911
non-emergency
— Upper Keys
852-3211
— Middle Keys
289-2430
— Key West
296-2424 or
1-800-273-2677
• Social Services
— Upper Keys
852-7125
— Middle Keys
289-6016
— Key West
292-3515

Federal Government
Alcohol, Tobacco and
Firearms, Bureau of
— Broward
305-356-7369
— Palm Beach County
407 835 8878
— Monroe and Dade
305-592-9967
• Coast Guard
— Broward
305-927-1611
— Palm Beach County
407-844-4470
— Dade
305-536-5641
— Monroe
— Upper Keys
305-664-4404
— Middle Keys
305-743-6778

— Key West
305-292-8800
• Federal Bureau of
Investigation
— Broward
305-524-4928
— Palm Beach County
407-833-7517
— Monroe and Dade
305-994-9101
• Federal Emergency
Management Agency
1-800-462-9029
— Washington, D.C.
202-646-2400
202-646-2500
202-646-4600
• National
Hurricane Center
305-666-4612 ■

INDEX

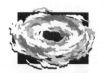

T

U

V

W

■

Here are some of the major sources used by the Sun-Sentinel for this book:

National Hurricane Center, Coral Gables, Fla.
Dade County Emergency Management Office, Miami.
Palm Beach County Emergency Management Office, West Palm Beach, Fla.
Broward County Division of Emergency Preparedness, Fort Lauderdale, Fla.
Broward County Social Services Division, Fort Lauderdale.
Monroe County Emergency Management, Key West, Fla.
National Oceanic and Atmospheric Administration, Washington, D.C.
University of Miami Rosenstiel School of Marine and Atmospheric Science, Miami.
William Gray, professor of atmospheric sciences, Colorado State University, Fort Collins, Colo.
U.S. Army Corps of Engineers, Washington.
Florida Power & Light Co.
Federal Emergency Management Agency, Washington.
Jay Baker, professor of geography, Florida State University, Tallahassee, Fla.
Sun-Sentinel Editorial Research Center, Fort Lauderdale.
American Red Cross.
"Florida Weather," by Morton D. Winsberg.
Everett Rawlings, owner, Federal Building Inspections, Boca Raton, Fla.
Palm Beach County Cooperative Extension Service, West Palm Beach.
Broward County Cooperative Extension Service, Davie, Fla.
Florida Attorney General's Office
Larry Schneider, architect, Currie, Schneider and Associates, Delray Beach, Fla.
Doug Andrews, utilities manager, Coral Springs, Fla.
Police Maj. Chuck Habermehl, Homestead, Fla.
Guardian Pools Inc., Davie, Fla.
American Automobile Association.
Sumter County Emergency Management Office, Sumter, S.C.
Florida Governor's Disaster Planning and Response Review Committee, Tallahassee.
Florida Solar Energy Center, Jacksonville, Fla.
Army-Navy Surplus store, Davie, Fla.
Michael Culotti, emotional trauma specialist, Family Enterprises Inc., Milwaukee, Wis.
Crisis Management International Inc., Atlanta.
The Associated Press.
Bob Haehle, horticulture consultant, Fort Lauderdale.
1992 Weather Guide Calendar, by The Weather Channel
Children's Television Workshop, New York.
University School of Nova University, Coral Springs.
Child Care Connection of Broward County, Fort Lauderdale.
"Atlantic Hurricanes," by Gordon Dunn.
Guaranteed Electronics Service, Hollywood, Fla.
Institute of Food and Agricultural Center, Hialeah, Fla.
Home Depot U.S.A., Pompano Beach, Fla.
Poulan/Weed Eater, Shreveport, La.
Insurance Information Institute, New York.
Folding Shutter Corp., West Palm Beach.

■

This book was made possible in large part by the extraordinary day-to-day coverage of Hurricane Andrew by the staff of the Sun-Sentinel, including:

Debbie Bradford, Connie Bramstedt, Joan Brookwell, Kevin Davis, Berta Delgado, Melinda Donnelly, Gordon Edes, Ellen Forman, Ardy Friedberg, William E. Gibson, John Gittelsohn, John Grogan, Margo Harakas, Deborah S. Hartz, John Hughes, Trevor Jensen, Kathleen Kernicky, Bob Knotts, Lyda Longa, Vicki McCash, Nancy McVicar, Don Melvin, Jill Young Miller, Buddy Nevins, Deborah Ramirez, Ray Recchi, Warren Richey, Fred Schulte, Glenn Singer, Ken Swart, Kathy Hensley Trumbull, Luisa Yanez, Michael E. Young.

■

PERSONAL NOTES

IMPORTANT
PHONE NUMBERS
Relatives, friends and
organizations in your area.

IMPORTANT POLICY NUMBERS

Automotive, boat, homeowner insurance policy numbers and agents.

_____

_____

_____

_____

_____

_____

_____

_____

_____

_____

_____

_____

_____

_____

_____

_____

_____

_____

_____